what people are saying abou

coming to your senses,
soaring with your soul

"REMARKABLE! A must-have guide to real life!"
—Erin Lafferty, *licensed massage therapist*

"Sally's voice is that of someone who truly validates honesty within the human heart. Her energy and passion flow throughout the book, and are contagious! In our fast-paced world, it is nice to take some time to BREATHE, to reflect, and to get back to yourself. This book helped me do just that."
—Michelle Matson, *home-schooling mother of four*

"This isn't a book, it's an experience. Its lessons become part of your being."
—Maurizio Miozza,
program manager of Italian manufacturing company

"*Coming to Your Senses* captured the ideas that I knew lay just beyond, but couldn't quite find words for. Now, every time I feel myself closing down, I hear Sally's exclamation – *Open!* – then completely readjust my physical body and mental mindset. Rather than feeling weighed down by the daily stress and negativity of my workplace, I feel like soaring into each new day, ready to greet the people and situations I encounter, confident that even the toughest moments won't keep me down for long."
—Beth Trinchero, *teacher*

"A fascinating combination—as luminous, playful, and provocatively radiant as its author!"
—Pamela Hanson, *singer-songwriter
and elementary school music teacher*

"If you want to be more open to the world of possibilities in any realm, read this book!"

—Jon Staenberg, *managing director, venture capital fund*

"The book is more of a feeling, rather than words. I'm tingling. I can feel the transformation, the new juices flowing. And I can feel my fears, too, but have a new relationship with them now. They no longer need to stop me. MAGIC!"

—Karen McElhinney, *operating room nurse*

"*Coming to Your Senses* doesn't give a #$%@ about my deep-seeded, issue-filled past . . . it cares about me in the present tense. I'm no longer Freud's little misfit or the child of divorced parents. I'm a beam of energy, with a few orbiting parasites to identify, evaluate, and either put into perspective or eliminate altogether. Simple."

—G. M. R., *graduate student*

"This book is practical, thought-provoking, and has convinced me that we have far more control over our energy than we thought possible!"

—Wendy Noritake, *magazine publisher*

"I had a lightbulb moment when I read Step 2 where you learn to get rid of things that drain your energy. I no longer feel obligated to hold onto things and friendships that suck the life out of me and consume my precious time. Best of all, Sally made me realize I didn't have to feel guilty about the elimination process. Thank you!"

—Sandra Watkins, *creative director*

"We weren't brought here to be rude and unkind to each other. We're here to be happy and make friends. That's really what this book is about, isn't it?"

—Juliet Dootson, *elementary school student*

"This book confirms what I've suspected all along: I'm really Italian at heart!"

—Michael Roche, *fine art photographer*

"Finally, a book about personal exploration and growth that shows the path clearly, without a lot of extraneous psychobabble."
—Lee W. Brillhart, *chairman and chief executive officer, defense contractor*

"If we could bottle its exuberance, we'd all be rich!"
—Juanita Gonzalez, *mother of two*

"Profoundly inspiring, uplifting, and empowering. The insights and techniques glow brilliantly with joy and creativity. A remarkable book!"
—Jamal Rahman, *Sufi teacher and author of* The Fragrance of Faith

"Fast paced, well written, high impact. I am working on the exercises, and read a little more each night! Sally's Chronic Fatigue Syndrome was different than mine, but the results of the illness still had the same impact on my life."
—Kelli Kassor, *small business owner*

"Like an acupuncturist for the soul, Sally Veillette helps you discover the root of whatever's holding you back and fundamentally change it. You'll learn dozens of fun, practical exercises that'll help you listen to your feelings and be flexible in the face of constant change. In other words, you'll learn how to be healthy. In our ideal state, instinct synchronizes with thought and is powered into action at a moment's notice."
—G.W. Winborn, *advertising copywriter*

"*Coming to Your Senses* delightfully lifts the veils that we use to hide from ourselves, and awakens us to our unabashed brilliance!"
—Gina Salà, *global vocalist and workshop facilitator*

"A must-read for burnt-out overachievers, disenfranchised dot-commers, stressed-out parents, displaced workers, and disillusioned bosses."
—Rosanne Siino, *Internet entrepreneur*

"WOW! Oh my, did you make me smile! We need your book in this world now, more than ever!"
—Brenda Lhormer, *Director, Cinema Epicuria,*
The Sonoma Valley Film Festival

"I haven't even finished the book, and already it has changed my life—honestly! I lead a very busy, very full life and I need every ounce of energy I can muster. *Coming to Your Senses* is helping me reclaim this most precious of all resources—the energy to do the things I really love!"
—Jill Hamilton, *mental health counselor and*
community activist

"Sally's humorous approach to what can be a daunting subject opened my curiosity. Her simple, thought-provoking style made the ideas flow. I defy anyone to read *Coming to Your Senses* and not feel more hopeful and at peace—on top of the world!"
—Kate Gerwe, *Internet executive*

"I find myself wanting to digest the book carefully and slowly, not rush through to the end to find the answers. Surprisingly, the slower I go, the more answers come, things I already knew, but hadn't taken the time to listen for before. I'm still reading it, re-reading it, digesting, practicing staying true to myself, and staying connected. Sally, your experience has been exquisitely recorded to benefit many of us who have lost our connection with ourselves. Thank you!"
—Colleen Kastan, *single mother and entrepreneur*

Coming to Your *Senses*

Soaring with Your Soul

Coming to Your Senses

Soaring with Your Soul

A Practical Guide

Sally M. Veillette

Brown Books Publishing Group
Dallas, Texas

For information, please contact:
Pop the Cork Publishing, L.L.C.
1629 McGilvra Blvd. East
Seattle, WA 98112
info@popthecorkpublishing.com
www.comingtoyoursenses.com

Produced for Pop the Cork Publishing by:
Brown Books Publishing Group
16200 North Dallas Pkwy., Suite 170
Dallas, Texas 75248
www.brownbooks.com
972-381-0009

Paperback: ISBN 0-9741854-1-8
        LCCN 2003109641
Casebound: ISBN 0-97-41854-0-X
        LCCN 2003107568
First Printing, 2003

To my daughter Chiara,
whose smile is this book's inseparable twin.

contents

coming to our senses

Ten years ago you'd have classified me as a classic American adrenaline junkie, leaping tall buildings in a single bound, at the top of the class in both high school and college, the golden girl at any office I'd worked in. I was also the one who had no idea who she was underneath the long list of accomplishments that grew with each passing day. I barely gave myself time to breathe before moving on to the next activity designed to please, serve, impress, or delight—*someone else.*

In late 1992, with the sudden onset of Chronic Fatigue Syndrome (CFS), my ability to power through life came to a screeching halt. For two-and-a-half long years, the illness stole my energy, scrambled my mind, sent pains through my body, and often left me so weak that I was unable to stand for five minutes at a time. *But it also proved to be the best friend I'd ever had.* It forced me to find the truer, more limit-less, energy source within me, a much more powerful and reliable one than the occasional boost I had previously gotten from the outside world in the form of compliments, approving nods, proud looks, promotions, and raises. I learned that in order to access this boundless energy, I simply had to reach in, clear a path for it to get to the surface, and it would perform—*for me.*

As a kid I always wondered why life had to be so hard—so much negativity, so many words that remained unsaid, and so many opportunities to comfort one another that passed by just for spite. Even during the good times we had (which were many), I'd stuff my stomach long past the point of being satisfied, and all too soon brace myself for the inevitable fights that were bound to pop up. With a confusing mixture of sensations around and within me, I sought refuge in life's rules and followed them religiously, doing exactly what I was expected to do.

What I'd discovered through my painful, persistent, and supportive teacher was a whole new game—a soulful, flexible framework to replace the old stagnant, rigid rules.

But as a thirty-two-year-old woman faced with an illness that had no known cause or cure, I'd run out of rules to follow. Suddenly my body had become my only guide: me, myself, and I against the world that I'd known those decades before. I was forced to open my heart and dive right in, digging through clutter, bursting through barricades, opening locked doors. For the first time in my life, I found myself putting myself first—being selfish, direct, and both brutally and refreshingly honest. It was contrary to everything I'd ever learned to be. I was on a huge scavenger hunt, fueled by necessity.

Luckily, it worked. With each passing season, my energy began to stabilize a little more—ten-minute labored walks in the park became easier, staircases less of a dread. I spent fewer hours in bed, was more effective at the manufacturing company where I'd worked, and my mind became clearer. The more I treated my illness as a friend and my body as a teacher, the less crippled I felt, and the easier it was to handle any problem that came my way. Rays of hope appeared, joining together to form rainbows. Life's ups and downs became a fun ride. My business grew and I made more money—as did many people around me. I couldn't believe it. One wasn't supposed to profit from such things.

What I'd discovered through my painful, persistent, and supportive teacher was a whole new game—a soulful, flexible framework to replace the old stagnant, rigid rules. And as a good engineer, I wanted to understand everything about it—each parameter, all the variables, every dynamic. Hence, I created this owner's manual for the soul.

do, be, create

The motivation for serious self-reflection is often the result of some kind of crisis: an illness, the loss of a job or relationship, or a goal reached without the expected happiness on the other side. Sometimes we are spurred on by an inner confusion, something percolating under the surface, a creeping feeling that life can be more than a collection of non-stop activities, achievements, and occasional awards. We may not know what to do next. We may feel lost, empty, and confused. But as uncomfortable as this can be, it is actually a very important experience.

Fueled by the kind of passion Hollywood has made famous, the hero wakes up from an ordinary life ready to suddenly challenge the status quo, confront the establishment, defy authority, and win. A partner walks out—*or in*—on a spouse, learning of an infidelity, then finally doing something about it. Someone reaches the top of the corporate ladder, then gives it all up for love. It's an exploding fury, a bursting through, breaking away, popping out, nothing short of a revolution.

In our normal lives, we use this kind of fiery passion during critical moments of change. We have that talk with our partner or boss, then get the new understanding, job transfer, or promotion we desire. We stretch ourselves and take a class, go to the movies alone, get a new haircut, or wear a different style of clothes. We may even start therapy, go to an introspective workshop, or read some spiritual self-help books. We show our partners how to better please us in bed. We travel to new neighborhoods, states, or countries. We blow off a week or weekend and take some time for ourselves instead. One way or another, we light the fire for something new to enter our lives.

This kind of passion is by nature destructive in its constructiveness, if you'll allow the paradox. It breaks through physical or mental barriers in order to open up new flows, allowing fresh ideas to come to light, giving the soul room to move. After the initial discomfort of the breakthrough (which is only natural), one is left with a sweet selfishness, an opening to more of the real you (which is equally natural). The daily "have to" activities become less important and relationships become more so as your spirit takes center ground. We breathe easily, and are happy smelling flowers and counting clouds in the sky. Colors take on a new vividness. Hearts open. Smells come alive. We move from "doing" to "being," after having proven that we possess the courage to do what's necessary to get there. Then we usually feel a strong urge to hang out there a bit, relaxing into the spaciousness, the insights, the fresh sensations, the peace, and the calm.

Do. Be. Create. The cycle of life. It starts with jam-packed activity and ends with jam-packed activity—the difference being that the primary motivation for our activities now emanates from within.

Paradoxically, just when we feel like we've gotten "being" down, we suddenly simply can't sit still. An urge bubbles up—the urge to create something, to connect with others, and to share our newly discovered selves. Whether it's channeled into our home lives, work, or hobbies, we find ourselves with a huge supply of energy to follow our cravings, to give in to our impulses, to scratch what's itching within. Our soul's on the move, moving us in its wake. It can be a bit scary at first. We don't want our lives to get over-scheduled, off-kilter, or out of control again. But the deeper kind of passion that is rising within us cannot be ignored. We *are* out of control, most definitely, but in a lovely and creative way.

The unenlightened may label us compulsive, but we know the difference between a distraction, vice, or numbing agent and what's boiling up under our skin. Ours is a *constructive* passion, freed from its prison by its *destructive* counterpart. It's a deep yearning, a sincere desire to express ourselves, to serve—and it comes with a free-flowing fountain of energy, a creative force that turns work to play.

Do. Be. Create. The cycle of life. It starts with jam-packed activity and ends with jam-packed activity—the difference being that the primary motivation for our activities now emanates from within. The cork pops off the bottle, freeing a path for creative passion to rise, and allowing the soul's force to surface through the highest level of our hearts. Vitality fills the air around us, lighting up our faces, and giving our bodies that undeniable glow—no matter what size our bank account or in what role we find ourselves.

digging up roots

When my "pop-through" moment came, I spread my wings wide, left the company that had been so good to me, and spent six months of each of the next six years on the road, exploring the minds, bodies, and souls of people of all titles, cultures, mindsets, shapes, and sizes.

I found no better place to root my work than Sicily, my big-breasted motherland where life is slower, personal connections are richer, and wine is served with every meal. You see, I was named after my grandfather, Salvatore, who'd been born there in 1899. He would have preferred that one of my two older brothers carry his name, as is the tradition, but "Sally" it was, and would be. I had no idea that a decision so seemingly random would turn out to be so appropriate, that I would be the only one of the four children in my family to stay in touch with our Italian roots and carry on my grandfather's tradition of dividing his time between the two worlds. Or that this very connection would be the catalyst to my exploration and eventual understanding of the human soul. As with many things in life, it happened by surprise.

My grandfather's old apartment is nestled on the southern shores of Sicily, facing Africa, where the calm waters of the Mediterranean Sea lap at its feet every minute of every day, and for some strange reason the locals arrive only in the summertime, leaving the beach town virtually deserted the other three seasons of the year. The sun rises to the left each morning and sets to the right each night, with the moon following the same path blazed by its predecessor. The lives of the people follow a similar daily cycle: the morning bustle, afternoon siesta, and resurgence of activity beginning around five o'clock, peaking at midnight, and waning until early dawn.

Becoming fluent in Italian took study, immersion, and practice. But I was also learning a new language of emotion, heart, and soul—something that required an equal amount of attention. I swear that the Italians actually feel their senses of sight, sound, taste, smell, and touch more deeply than we Americans do. If they cut themselves, I bet it hurts more. When they put a bite of food in their mouths, I suspect the taste is more pungent for them than it is for us. A *puzza* (bad smell) bothers them more than it does us. They see the beauty in a work of art or in nature more directly than we do. It moves them in ways we can only hope to understand. They feel more. I'm convinced of it.

Life to them is not skin-deep. In fact, there is so much physical beauty in the country that it doesn't carry the weight that it does here. The presence of it doesn't give you an instant entry into one crowd, and the lack of it doesn't exclude you from another. It's just one aspect of a person, one of many.

Young, old, disfigured, or disabled—all are free to be seen in Sicily, to take the nightly evening stroll, *la passeggiata,* and to participate in the community. My Italian friends often ask me where we hide our older people, why we lock them up in retirement homes or confine them to certain southern states. Life is not real to Italians without the full range of ages, tastes, scents, flavors, and the complete spectrum of human forms that exist.

One friend, after having visited me in Sicily for ten days or so, found that she was having trouble looking people in the eyes. "They see too much of me," she said, turning her eyes away even from mine. Being a forty-year-old woman who'd had the habit of hiding behind fifty or so extra pounds of weight for most of her adult life, the realization that this weight wasn't keeping the Sicilians from seeing who she really was was a bit much for her to handle. As they responded to her beauty, she was being asked to do the same—something quite new and uncomfortable for her.

There is no hiding in Sicily, nor should there be anywhere else in the world. Each of us has a unique melody to sing—that, in my opinion, it is our *responsibility* to sing, at the command of our very souls. It's precisely the combination of these melodies that makes the world go round. A symphony would be no fun to listen to if it were filled with only clarinets. A football team of all halfbacks wouldn't get very far. The world couldn't grow and change if children were just cookie-cutter copies of their parents. We each bring something to the table, an individual thread for the tapestry, a distinct voice for the choir. Nothing, absolutely nothing, in nature is wasted. Somewhere inside we each have an inner glow that is waiting to come to the surface, a passion that's ready to fuel even the most mundane of our days.

utopia

Do I expect that by the end of this book, we will reach utopia, a life of 10,000 watt shines, blue skies, and unrushed days? Absolutely not. In fact, a genuine imperfection is our goal. Clear connections, a crisp focus, souls at play. Except, of course, on the days they're not . . . those days that deflate us, confound us, and send us running for the hills. What I can promise, though, is that we'll have a much better perspective by the book's end, much more comfort with our own humanity, and learn to use even the worst of our days to our advantage. Shrinking from them—*or anything*—will seem like a less valid option. We'll discover the superpowers of a perfectly imperfect human being.

Hollywood has many of us convinced that each day is supposed to be bright and sunny, and that each story needs an appropriately happy ending. The Italians call this *"americanata,"* then roll their eyes, and turn off the TV. But to many Americans, unless our lives are perfect in this exaggerated way, we are convinced that they need to be fixed. Continuous improvement projects flourish in every downtown office. We have tens of thousands of self-help books. But do we really need all of this? Maybe an unabashed opening to our realness is the magic key that will relax our brains, stir our souls, and make room for our vitality to pop through—paradoxically bringing a bigness and brightness to our inner view of ourselves and a super-human spring to our step.

We can have an abundance of energy, you know. It's perfectly natural.

A young woman recently confided to me that she has one or two pretty bad days every month and wondered what was wrong—not because there were too many, but because there were too few. She thought that perhaps she was manic and needed a medicine to bring her down. Being too happy concerned her; it made her different. Depression, she thought, was more fitting a good graduate student.

"Pay me the $100 an hour," I offered, "and I'll assure you you're just fine. You've got the life people dream of . . . fueled by your very own fire. Yes, you are different. You do an unusual assortment of things and have a unique look. And I can see by one glance that you're filling your day with things you really love, and that they feed you. You've made it, my dear. At twenty-eight years old, you already have what everyone seeks."

I really believe that we *can* have it all: vibrant rich lives as unique to each of us as we are to the world. Mania comes from a disconnection with what we know as true. Burn-out comes from using an unclean fuel. When we are powered by our true selves, we not only work more efficiently, but work becomes fun. Our energy climbs. Everyday duties stop weighing us down. Risks become comfortable as our souls become well-trained in opening after having tightened up with worry and stress. When we reopen enough times, our movements begin to mirror that of a bird's wing—*contract, expand, contract, expand*—and we take flight. Then with our wings spread wide, we give up the struggle, let the wind support us, and soar across even the highest mountaintops. A breeze is in our faces. Fresh air is in our lungs. Our view is immense. We know who we are, and as a friend of mine puts it, "We've got our glow on."

Through the eight steps in this book we bring these words down from the skies to experience them here on earth in a most direct way.

the approach

This isn't your normal self-help book. It's a "help-yourself-to-yourself" book. The days of concentrating on what's wrong with us are gone. The days of moving with what's right with us have finally arrived. And the key is to feel very deeply what we really,

really, really feel inside, skillfully bypassing the rat's nest of emotions, tensions, and awkward sensations and arriving at the bold, simple, and pure truth. By clearing the path to let our whole selves out, we unclog our pipes and encourage our souls to take a greater role in steering our days. A bit of disassembly of habits that numb, politeness that binds, and thoughts that constrict is required to stoke our inner flames until a nice healthy glow takes permanent hold—shaving years off our looks, putting a bounce in our steps, and giving us the discernment to make choices aligned from within.

In the first two chapters, I offer my personal story as a way for you to get to know me a little better and as a concrete example of what a soul looks like when it's on the move.

As you read this story, don't get distracted by the fact that an illness was at its core. Look beyond the illness itself to the push-pull of the soul's movement bubbling up from within. View it, if you can, as a "good" thing. See if you can spot how my soul spoke through my symptoms. Notice how my inner voice rose up in an attempt to unsettle an outer world that had grown a bit disconnected from a clear inner view of itself, too rigid in its approach, and less-than-soulfully-honest in the motivation behind its choices. Spot the number of times I'd felt a true feeling rise up through the chaos, then pushed it back down either out of habit, confusion, or fear . . . or simply because I'd had a different idea of my direction and didn't want to entertain any other options. That's the soul's *push-pull,* the voice of our real selves, fighting to be heard.

Watch as I awaken to my soul's inner movement and begin to give it more and more room to breathe, inviting it to talk to me directly. Instead of forcing my soul to squeeze itself up through a crack in a barren sidewalk, I give it a full garden, a playground, center stage.

Finally, keep one of your inner eyes on the big picture that unfolds around me, the way each detailed movement comes together to create a coordinated dance, perfectly orchestrated, but graceful only when I open myself to its embrace.

The magic of this process is in the gentle opening that each step provides. It is precisely the gentleness and thoroughness of each opening that holds this book's power.

After the personal story, I offer eight steps to help-yourself-to-yourself. Simple steps. Hundreds of exercises. To be done in any order you choose. And you don't need to leave your job as I did or drop everything and travel the world. You can stay put and fly just the same. As Dorothy discovered, "There's no place like home." The steps in this book can be done from your favorite armchair. And each chapter leads you one distinct step closer to attaining that year-round tan, that undeniable inner glow that lights up your world and the lives of everyone you touch—*naturally.*

Let any fear of flying simply disappear. These steps are manageable. Each is just a small distance from the one that came before it and, when joined together, form a framework of the soul's movement, a treasure map to the mix of feelings we have within. Each contains a wealth of playful exercises, more than anyone can possibly do. I call them "games" because they are light and fun. They provide something for everyone, as a great playground should, approaching each step's subject matter from many directions, providing insightful exercises, introspective meditations, and physical activities from which to choose.

The magic of this process is in the gentle opening that each step provides. It is precisely the gentleness and thoroughness of each opening that holds this book's power. You can do the steps in any order you'd like. But do only the steps that draw you to them, that entice you, and stimulate your curiosity. Before you know it, with no "work" at all, you will find your perspective

shifting, old habits breaking, new energy rising, and new options appearing. By the book's end, your soul will be freed to work at it full feeling and creative capacity.

This book, like life, has many options of how to approach it. And the approach that it offers is both rich and generous, both powerful and tender at the same time. I hope you have as much fun with it as it wants to have with you.

soul maintenance

The care, feeding, and alignment of the soul

STEP 1, FEEL
Come back to your senses.

STEP 2, CLEAN
Clean off who you aren't.

STEP 3, POLISH
Shine up who you are.

STEP 4, WALK
Stay yourself more each day.

these steps are for you
do with them what you will

I designed these steps as less of a ladder and more of a framework, a step-by-step view of the magical dynamics of the soul. Consequently, you have ultimate freedom in how they're used. You don't have to begin at the beginning, just flip through them and pick where to enter. Then choose how many or how few you want to do.

The steps are structured in two sets of four each: 1 to 4, and 5 to 8.

steps 1 to 4
SOUL MAINTENANCE. Feel who you are and who you aren't, and realign with the most real you that you can find. You will clean up your life, polish your shine, oil your squeaky spots, and step out into the world more authentically.

steps 5 to 8

SOUL MOVEMENT. Dive straight into the soul, learn its most basic open-close movement, and begin to recognize this dynamic in all that you do. By the book's end, you'll open yourself so wide that your passion simply pops out, moving you along with it.

If you like to start at the beginning of something, turn the page to Step 1, where you'll be encouraged to play with your feeling nature, and proceed from there. If you feel like you already have a pretty clear idea of who you are, you may want to jump directly to Step 5. Or you can enter the steps at random, then move around as you'd like. Or close the book, then reopen it, and start there. Or give all eight steps a quick read-through, then go back to what intrigues you most. By the way, it's common to have one or two steps that stick with you, demanding more attention, calling your name.

There are a wealth of exercises for each step and wide margins to write your answers in. Think of the exercises as "games" in the giant playground of life. Some people like to just read them, breathe when I suggest it, and wiggle their toes. Others whip out extra paper and a pen and jot down page after page of thoughts. As with life, each choice is yours.

Whatever choice you make, have fun with it. That's the most important thing of all.

---

soul movement
Steering life directly
from the soul

STEP 5, DIVE
Touch your soul.

STEP 6, FLY
Build your energetic
muscles and take flight.

STEP 7, SOAR
Give up the effort and
soar with the wind.

STEP 8, GLOW
Partner with your
inner passions.

living by
the numbers

On December 1, 1992, I came down with an illness that western medicine could barely identify, let alone cure. It was a sniper, a rogue, a clandestine enemy that I couldn't shake no matter how hard I tried. And believe me, I tried everything. In a moment of desperation, I even tried not trying anything at all and magically stumbled across a golden key, the answer to a question I'd been struggling with my whole life but thought could never be answered—*who the hell am I?* The internal struggles, confusing voices, urges, anxieties, drives, and fears were finally sorted out. And the inner knowing, the inkling that life just didn't have to be so complicated, so demeaning, so hard, was at last confirmed. Everything became clear.

But I'm getting ahead of myself, jumping to the pot of gold at the end of the rainbow. We're here at the beginning, and at the beginning we shall be. Let's dive into the heart, mind, and soul of the adrenaline junkie that I was: the Sally before Sally knew what Sally was meant to be. Some of you may have forgotten that there is a place for a heart and soul in our lives, not to mention in our business worlds, so perhaps I should back up even more. Let's start at the top, shall we? In the human head. It's the center of our thoughts, the part (of me, at least) that's programmed to produce, that's willing to go to the wall in the name of achievement, to push past any inner urges to slow down, any craving to connect, and any suggestion to soften. Yes, that's the perfect place for this story to begin.

The old Sally lived in her head, by the numbers, constantly calculating achievements, deadlines, and timelines. In the year before I got sick, in fact, I closed the largest order in the history of the company, twice as big as anything we'd dared to dream before, over twenty-two times the size of a normal satisfying catch. It was a successful conclusion to an intense six-month effort. And within minutes of the announcement, I was already on to the next goal, pissed off that the rest of the team was wasting precious time congratulating one another. We had better things to do. The smile that I'd put on my face for the occasion grew weary as I waited for the group to refocus, a familiar pressure building to a climactic fury inside my brain.

I was Jell-O without a mold, Cinderella at the stroke after midnight, Hansel and Gretel in the woods after the birds had eaten all the bread crumbs . . . undeniably and reliably lost.

That year I'd been in the best physical shape of my life—133 pounds of lean muscle on an athletic five-foot-six-inch frame. My bones had only hard muscles to pad them, long having left any softer tissue behind. I'd recently climbed Mount Rainier—danced the 14,410 feet to the top, in fact—and no sooner had returned to sea level than begun rigorously training a solid two-and-a-half hours a day for triathlons.

In the days before I got sick, I'd brought a new boyfriend across the country to meet my family over Thanksgiving, looking for approval, but finding rejection instead. Confused, I was sitting alone on a plane headed back to Seattle, alternately leaning my head against the window and scribbling notes in my journal, as my mind began to twist around itself. The old formulas I'd lived by just didn't add up. I was Jell-O without a mold, Cinderella at the stroke after midnight,

Hansel and Gretel in the woods after the birds had eaten all the bread crumbs . . . undeniably and reliably lost.

That's the moment Chronic Fatigue Syndrome found its way in. Most people who've had this illness can vividly remember the day it arrived. Being the overachiever that I am, I remember the very instant. It felt like something snapped, a twang twanged, a plug unplugged, a circuit shorted somewhere deep inside me. The sensation was inside, but as was my habit back then, I searched outside for the explanation, looking over my shoulder to see if something or someone was there. It was a curious move, considering I was 35,000 feet above the earth in a window seat of a United Airlines plane.

Seeing nothing unusual, I wiped the tears from my face and reread my journal entries. It'd been an odd year, one of extremes. I'd achieved more than I'd ever expected to, checked off every box on my list, but was more miserable than ever.

Pulling my gaze from the clouds outside the airplane window, I focused on the last paragraph I'd written. *I feel like a blob of protoplasm with no backbone, no self-defined ideas. Without my family around me, it is worse. I am nothing.*

Scenes of how I'd shaped my life around my family flashed through my mind. The big things: which degrees to get, which jobs to take, or which guys to date. The tiny things like the smiles that I'd plastered on my face at just the right times, the 24/7 scan of moods that had formed my cue for action, the scripts in which my conversations had so often been contained.

Then, in a kind of moment that's both a gift and a curse all rolled into one, I realized my life was being lived for someone else—for my boss, my boyfriend, my family, my friends. I was mysteriously absent from my very own life. Right then, if you'd asked me about the positive parts of my daily activities and relationships (of which there were many indeed), I don't think

I'd have been able to tell you even one. The force of how I'd been faking life filled me and cut my breath short, its concentration sending a shock wave through my system that defied the numbers, tumbled down my house of cards, and sent Humpty Dumpty shattering into pieces below. *Who in the world was I?* I had no idea.

a first step

When I stepped off the plane in Seattle, it felt like I'd contracted a bad flu. My muscles ached, my throat was sore, my eyes watered, and my head swam. I was exhausted.

I pushed through my daily routine, trying hard to ignore the annoying (and increasing) symptoms of my illness. One day, leafing through a stack of mail with my left hand while dialing the doctor's office with my right, I saw that the graduate school applications from both Harvard and Stanford business schools had arrived. As the nurse was calling in the antibiotic prescription (after all, it was just a little case of the flu, right?), I tore open the applications.

Yes, I thought, going to grad school was exactly what I needed: a well-timed and welcome relief. Besides, I'd been frustrated with my company for not following through on the promises we'd made our customers. And I'd been furious at my manager for giving me a lukewarm performance review, having marked me down in "teamwork" of all things. The support staff had complained that I'd been too demanding. If they wanted to feel pressure, I thought, why didn't they try living in my shoes for a while? That'd give them something to complain about.

Over Christmas break, when my mysterious "flu" allowed me to concentrate, I tackled the applications. Harvard's was as well-organized and logical as I'd expected. It asked for details of each accomplishment, award, and honor, and specified the exact amount of space I could dedicate to each essay—a strict half page. My competitive juices flowed as I packed as much into each little box as I possibly could, following each rule with machine-like precision.

When I started on Stanford's, I was immediately struck by the contrast. The section on credentials was short and sweet, a breeze after having done Harvard's. For the essays, not only did they not place a limit on their length, their questions had little or nothing to do with what I'd accomplished or with how many and which goals I'd achieved.

A wave of curiosity swept over me and my mind raced not forward, but inward, then paused to open like a flower in spring. My symptoms took a backseat as the *"who am I?"* question that had been dancing around my brain for almost a month now, appeared once again in front of me, in black and white, demanding my undivided attention. Or, as Stanford more elegantly phrased it, *"Each of us has been influenced by the people, events, and situations of our lives. How have these influences shaped who you are today? (Our goal is to get a sense of who you are, rather than what you've done.)"*

True to form, I started the essay with statistics, happy to have found a comfortable way to begin. In 1992, I wrote, I'd accumulated 37,888 frequent flier miles on business trips between Seattle and California, made over 6,500 phone calls, booked $8,103,900 of new business for our company, and received an 18 percent raise. I skied 78 hours, hiked 41,420 vertical feet, swam 792 laps, spent 28 hours on the Stairmaster, biked 347 miles, ran 208 miles, and lifted over 485,000 pounds. I refinished 28 antique picture frames, took 252 pictures, had 192 friends over for dinner, went on 107 dates, sold 151 tickets to a local dance company's concerts as the head of its volunteer team, and read over 4,000 pages. I spent 312 hours with my family on the east coast, 576 hours with my friends across the country, passed mile 137,338 on my 1983 Toyota Tercel, saved $6,833.69 toward my emergency cash fund, wrote 92 pages in my journal, and sent 148 Christmas cards.

I'd started the compilation in a playful mood, but as I reread the snapshot of my life, my mind took a sudden self-critical spiral as I realized that I'd probably done *more* the year before. Why hadn't I applied last year, I thought. I felt exposed as a failure, naked in a crowded room of grad school applicants. Certainly Stanford would sense my downward slide. As my heart emptied itself of hope, the energy quickly drained from my body, and my sore throat and muscle aches flared.

Three days, ten pages, and several pizzas later, I completed the application, the first step in discovering who the real Sally was.

the roller coaster

At the dawn of the new year I was still pushing past my symptoms to get things done, assuming that I was just part of the half of Seattle that was down with the flu. I called for another round of antibiotics, but the nurse insisted that I come in instead. But after spending a full forty-five minutes in the overflowing waiting room, I was so mad at the waste of precious time that I could barely remember why I'd made the appointment in the first place.

Two weeks later, after my body aches surged and my mind raced late into the night, I called my best friend Jessica. She took me to the emergency room first thing the next morning, then received many desperate phone calls from me during the full week I spent in bed, barely able to move. Back to the doctor's office I went.

"I just called, and you said you could fit me in," I said.

"Certainly," the receptionist automatically replied, her head buried in the pages of the appointment book. When she looked up at me, her face went white.

Within a few short minutes the doctor himself came out to escort me back to an examining room. His nurse motioned for me to lie back on the table, put a blanket over me to calm my chills, and turned out the light. After the examination, a technician from the lab came in to draw some blood. I remember thinking that I must have looked pretty bad to get such special treatment. It was all kind of a dream.

Each day was a battle inside my very own skin. I was bright but couldn't concentrate. Exhausted, but couldn't get a good night's sleep. I'd have energy one minute and lose it the next.

"Daddy's little actress," my family used to call me. But on that day, I couldn't even fake it. My mind was peacefully parked in a bank of fog, on a break from its nonstop calculations, uninterested in controlling its outer world. Finally my doctor could see that something was really, really wrong indeed. All masks were off, exposing the vulnerability I'd been trying so hard to keep at bay. I was completely disconnected—both from the old Sally and from the Sally that my soul wanted me to be.

Still without an official diagnosis or treatment plan, over the next weeks I worked short hours each day, arriving late and leaving early, causing more than a few heads to turn.

Each day was a battle inside my very own skin. I was bright but couldn't concentrate. Exhausted, but couldn't get a good night's sleep. I'd have energy one minute and lose it the next. If I exercised, the fatigue wouldn't come immediately as with normal people, but the next morning . . . and in an exaggerated fashion. The confusion was becoming routine.

One night Jessica brought over some dinner. "Sally, it's the weirdest thing," she said. "Just now, your face seemed to change colors, like a wave had swept through it, going from pale to paler, if that's possible. Then I saw your eyes go blank and come back to life. There it is again. It's doing it again. That's got to be the most terrifying thing I've ever seen."

We sat there for a few minutes, Jessica watching the show with horror, before she helped me to my room.

Winter turned to spring. I hated every minute of it. I wanted my old life back—my energy and drive to accomplish anything I set out to do.

Late one afternoon, I picked up the phone to call a friend for a referral to another doctor, someone who might be able to diagnose what was going on with me. I'd planned to steady my voice and sound as calm as possible. But my attempt failed even before the first words came out of my mouth; I sobbed hysterically instead. All I could do was say, over and over again, how scared I was. That I had no idea what was wrong with me. That it hurt so much I wanted to die.

A specialist at a teaching hospital met with me for over two hours before making his diagnosis. He warned that CFS had no known cause or cure, explaining that it was a syndrome, a series of seemingly unrelated symptoms that were seen together enough times to form a distinct pattern. In the case of CFS, the pattern was an unexplainable fatigue that stayed with a person for a minimum of six months, that didn't resolve with bed rest, and that reduced daily activity by at least fifty percent.

At last I had a label and could form an action plan. I started by counting megadoses of vitamins each week and placing them in tiny plastic baggies that I'd found in a stamp-collecting store. One for the morning, one for mid-day, and one to have with the evening meal. A few weeks later, I added a huge bag of raw vegetables to the daily mix.

easy does it

Jessica's wedding date approached. Although I'd cancelled all but the most vital business trips to conserve my energy, I made plans to fly to New York for the ceremony. I called a friend in Manhattan to tell him I'd be in town.

"Come on, Sally, don't take this CFS thing so hard. *Relax, you deserve it,*" he said. "Take a break for a while."

I was speechless. I'd never even once considered giving in to this thing. Never. Not in a million years. But in a wave of emotion even more surprising than his words, tears streamed down my face, as the voice of what I would learn was my soul began to stir. Imagine suggesting that I relax, that I deserved a break. Me, who got up in the morning, turned my engine on high, and played superwoman for the rest of the day. Me, who fell exhausted into bed each night, without a drop of energy left to spare. To relax was both unthinkable . . . and secretly what I wanted more than anything else in the world.

"*Relax?*" I replied. Even the word sounded funny as it rolled off my tongue.

"Yeah. Relax." His response was more of a command than a suggestion.

Being the good engineer that I am, I devised an experiment: I would "relax" with a cup of tea each day for a week. My aunt seemed to enjoy it; surely I would, too. So I taped seven tea bags to my bedroom door. Each morning I peeled off one, boiled the water, and sat with my steaming cup at the picnic table on my back deck. And I probably don't have to tell you that more than once I caught myself getting up before my cup was finished, in a rush to get on with my day.

But to my credit, I must say that by the fourth or fifth cup I did notice the purple wisteria beginning to bud on the veranda, a plant that I'd never before realized was even there.

And with the seventh cup, I decided to consider more seriously my doctor's suggestion to take the summer off before starting graduate school. This marked the first real victory in the push-pull war that my soul and stubbornness were having inside my skin.

While in New York for Jessica's wedding, I had another cup of tea, this time with an old childhood friend. Her father, a psychologist, offered to help me sort out some of my feelings. Dr. Rapoport looked me squarely in the eyes, took my hands in his, and said, "Sally, put down your external priorities and toolbox of survival tactics. Put them down. You cannot just *survive* anymore. You need to change your motivation from externally-based to internally-based, to one that is nurturing to you.

"Remove all external forces and discover who you are. Become a waitress if you need to. You are a master of acting and serving others. You need to learn how to *feel*, not *do*—to feel and own all parts of yourself, to nurture the little girl inside of you, the one that was never allowed to be little before.

"Do things she'll like. You're an artist. Draw her out with laughter, color, creativity. Let her play. Drop out of sight to bring her into sight. You need her to become whole. Try to get in touch with yourself and your human capacity to love."

In the short time we spent together that afternoon we covered what would ordinarily take about two years in therapy. Indeed, it would take me the rest of the two years to really understand and digest what he meant. *Feel, not do. Switch from external to internal motivation. Get in touch with the human capacity to love.* These thoughts swirled around in my brain, trying to find a home, as I watched Jessica walk down the aisle, glowing in that special way that at the time I thought only brides could do.

Later that week I felt a glow rising up inside myself, lulled into a peaceful trance by the ancient philosophy book, the *Tao Te Ching*. Its eighty-one poems describe life as a river and teased me with the notion that a varied, twisty, curvy path like a river's brings life alive. Efficient, precise, assured paths were dry and bland by comparison.

When I returned again to Seattle, a friend noticed how serene I'd become and panicked. "This isn't Sally!" he said. "Sally is vibrant and full of intense energy! Don't you change on me!" Startled by his response, I popped back into my old world, not having a firm enough footing in the new one to stay there. Strike up a "loss" in the battle in my skin.

changing roles

When the acceptance letters arrived from the graduate schools, I decided both to go to Stanford and to follow the doctor's suggestion to take the summer off. Little did I know that within a month, the president of our company would offer me the position of general manager of a newly-formed division— with no additional degree required.

I turned him down flat. Stanford University was where I wanted to be. An oasis in the desert and a change of pace for me. Enter a "win" for steering from within.

Ten minutes later, the phone rang. It was the director of human resources, determined to talk me into accepting the position. "Sally, I don't think anyone from this company has ever said this before, but I'm going to," she said. "I've been watching you over the past two years. I've seen you break through roadblock after roadblock until you brought in that new major account. As managers, we should have removed the roadblocks so you could fly. Instead, we just put up higher ones to see if you could get over those, too. As general manager,

Sally, *you* can define the rules. You can open doors for your group and watch them fly. You can right the wrongs."

I was confused. Her words were like nothing I'd heard from a businessperson before. They pierced my skin, making me question if my rejection of their offer had really been a "win." Tears instantly welled up, wielding a force that took all of my energy and will to control.

The president's appeal to me had been through his head, businessperson-to-businessperson. He'd practically dictated how my new resume entry would read. The human resources director worked with a much greater power—clearing a path for my business life to become less of a struggle, and for my inner creativity to have room to breathe. She transported me beyond my own small self and offered the chance to help others turn work into play, too. I'd never actually experienced work as play before, but somehow still knew that it was possible. My heart jumped at the chance to prove this was true.

It took my head some time, though, to catch up and agree—one month to be exact. My only condition was that I get Wednesdays off. There was no way I could work five full days in a row until my health stabilized. So Stanford was out, and the general manager position was in. And the war inside my skin? I wasn't sure if it was a score for my soul or my resume. Only time would tell for sure.

On my first free Wednesday I went to a Chinese herbalist—a bit out of my element at the time, but I was willing to try anything to find a quick, miraculous end to my illness. What I got instead was a full day of brewing, straining, and stirring a huge pile of smelly herbs that looked like scrapings from the bottom of a forest floor. And a wave of nausea so strong that I practically threw up as I tried to down the greenish-black, tar-like fluid.

The next Wednesday I visited an acupuncturist, literally dragging myself to her office and up a flight of stairs that seemed like ten, down a hall that felt a mile long, then into an office filled with odd smells and sounds. She asked me to stick out my tongue (both up and down) and reveal my pulses (on both wrists) so she could make the decision as to which of the 324 acupuncture points on my body she was going to stick needles into. She picked sixteen.

Luckily, before she agreed to treat me, she'd made me promise to come a minimum of six times to give the treatments a chance; otherwise I might never have set foot into that office again. It took eight sessions before I felt anything at all. Then, all at once, a wave went through my body, flushing away in one smooth movement the flu-like aches that had plagued my muscles for nine full months. It was as if my muscles had been holding their breath and finally let go in one gigantic exhale.

That was the first real relief I'd had from my symptoms. The muscle aches came and went regularly after that, but they didn't stick around for any extended period of time. I couldn't argue with the success, though I didn't understand it one bit.

The fall passed quickly and winter arrived. My symptoms were familiar enough to me that I knew how to push past them for at least a few hours each day to get done what I wanted, much like an athlete pushes past the pain for the sweet rush of endorphins. I would perform at meetings like an actress on a stage, a marionette enlivened for the show. Then in the evenings and on my Wednesdays, I'd crumble into a lifeless pile out of sight of the audience. The push-pull of my inner war was becoming a part of my being.

down the rabbit hole

As Christmas approached, I couldn't bring myself to buy a plane ticket to the east coast to visit my family. All the energy drained out of my body whenever I so much as thought about it . . . the long trip, the holiday crowds, the unpredictable weather, and the stress of a family get-together. I just couldn't do it. After weeks of stalling I told my family. Their reaction was ice cold, crystal clear, and predictable. I'd betrayed them and they didn't like it one bit.

You see, I'd never disobeyed my family before, let alone put my needs over their time-honored traditions. My head spun with a tension I couldn't control, revving up my symptoms, distorting my thoughts, and causing me to go cross-country skiing so I could fantasize that I was back to myself and would never disappoint anyone ever again.

Not surprisingly, I had a major relapse. Every symptom flared in the grandest of glory, robbing me of the ability to even stand for more than a few minutes at a time. I remember looking at the dishes in the sink and being absolutely stupefied at how one would go about washing them. I could have been offered a million dollars as payment

I had entered the mystery of mysteries, taken a step into the unknown, a plunge into the ocean of my soul.

and still not have figured out how to complete that simple, mundane task.

I sat in my armchair and began to cry. Even that was exhausting. I might as well face it, I thought, my life was over. I wouldn't be able to keep my job for much longer. And a family of my own? No way. For the second time since the illness began, I felt like I wanted to die, but couldn't imagine how to do that either. I just sat there and wept.

After crying myself out, I threw a video from a recent CFS conference into the VCR. I could barely understand a word the doctor was saying, so I busied myself by looking at the colorful brain scans of his patients. He showed scan after scan after scan, as his voice rambled on and on, and I blankly stared at the screen.

Suddenly something clicked, and my view of the colorful images quite literally flipped. The pictures made it all so clear. Slide after slide showed the same damaged areas . . . *and the same clear ones, completely unaffected by the illness.* In fact, the clear areas far outnumbered the damaged ones. The vast majority of the brain looked just fine. Perhaps a way out could be found, I reasoned, if I concentrated on the parts that still worked instead of insisting on returning to what didn't. Maybe my illness was supposed to win the fight over control of my body and show me a new way of approaching my days. Maybe it wasn't my enemy at all. Maybe it was my friend.

In that instant, on January 2, 1994, I made the choice to start a new life—ignoring what didn't work and experimenting with what might. I was Alice going down the rabbit hole or Milo taking his toy car through the phantom tollbooth. I could feel a wisp of energy rise up inside my fragile body. I felt anxious, it's true, but an anxiety born of joy rather than pressure, trust rather than fear. I had entered the mystery of mysteries, taken a step into the unknown, a plunge into the ocean of my soul. My soul hummed gently in response, quite content at its clear victory.

My road would take many more twists and turns over the nine months before my symptoms would begin to turn around, and the six more months it would take to be completely cured. And over that time, I would slowly and surely become an expert in my body's language and how it communicates my soul's truest desires.

The fact is that each of us has all we need to make our way through life, moving with it rather than against it. Within our own bodies, we have a friend, an ally, a confidant, a guide.

As we learn to trust in this soulful connection, as we open to it, we feel its truth, and draw a pure power from it to steer and fuel our days. That's what being real is all about—breathing, smelling, seeing, tasting, touching, and experiencing . . . *yourself.* And your reward? More vitality every step of the way.

lightening up

It's funny how after thirty-one years of perfecting the strive-surpass-achieve-please-adrenaline-junkie routine, thirteen long months of intensely fighting an illness that had no known cause or cure, it took but one instant to flip it all around. You could say that I'd decided to think positively, to play the hand I was dealt, to stop calculating the precise number of ounces in my cup, and simply view it as mostly full. But even those words fall short of the profound nature of the single split-second shift that sent me down the rabbit hole into a whole new world.

In that critical moment, the moment that I watched that silly video and the anything-but-silly insight popped out, *I decided to live*—regardless of knowing exactly what that life was going to look like. Instead of concentrating on the ways that my illness was limiting me, keeping me from being the "Sally" that I'd known, I looked at what it was *allowing* me to do. Thus ended my internal battles and began a life that bubbled up from within.

A big note saying *"I Surrender!"* decorated my refrigerator door, right next to the *"Relax, You Deserve It!"* sign that had been up there on and off for months, the occasional victim of a wave of sadness, pang of guilt, or fit of rage. Both signs were there to stay. I'd exchanged the bucking bronco for a magical carpet ride.

Each day was an adventure into the unknown. As I loosened up on my living-by-the-numbers orientation, I discovered a whole new me. I had a stunning acuity for the big picture, for brainstorming, for visual images and concepts. I could set strategies and direction that others couldn't even see. I could do a 1,000-piece jigsaw puzzle with ease. I could be poetic and profound. I could paint pictures to express ideas.

Maybe Dr. Rapoport was right. Maybe I was an artist, not only an engineer.

an alternative perspective

I still had a long, long way to go for my tired, stressed-out body to catch up with my expanded mental view. I decided to explore the world of complementary medicine more deeply, this time with a special kind of chiropractor whose name was given to me by a friend. *Please help me,* I thought, as I steadied myself on his treatment table, too weak to be curious about what was going to happen next or even to be the tiniest bit annoyed by the fact that I hadn't understood more than a few minutes of the instructional video I'd just watched.

The chiropractor asked me to hold out my right arm and think about the word "yes" as he pushed down on my arm to test its muscle strength. My arm remained strong to his touch. When I put the word "no" in my brain, by contrast, he was able to push down my arm with just a gentle touch of his hand. No matter how hard I tried, there was no way I could keep strength in it as long as there was that "no" in my brain. The mind-body reaction of this "applied kinesiology" technique was instantaneous. It spoke volumes about the physical perils of negative thoughts and gave me even more motivation to think of my illness as a "positive" thing.

That test complete, we began the treatment. He asked me

to hold out my arm and think about something stressful. I thought about CFS. He pushed with the same light force and my arm practically fell to the ground. It was like I didn't have any muscle at all.

"That's it," he said, matter-of-factly, then rummaged around my back and neck until he found two spots he seemed to like. I noticed that they were quite tender to the touch. He asked me to hold my breath. A few moments later, he told me to release it. When he rubbed the spots that he'd been touching, they weren't sore anymore. We repeated this process another few times, until for some reason he stopped and tested my arm strength again.

"Think about that same stressful situation," he instructed. This time my arm stayed strong, solid as a rock, thoughts of CFS and all.

"Muscle testing allows me to tap into your body's innate intelligence," he explained. "I get your brain (and mine) out of the way—our cultural training, so to speak. In this case, a few internal signals were mixed up. Don't worry, we got them straightened out today."

That night, for the first time since the illness had begun, I slept like a rock.

The next day when the chiropractor asked me to think of something stressful, I thought again of CFS. But my arm stayed strong; the layer of stress we'd removed had remained clear. The next stressful thing that came to mind was the image of that ill-fated Thanksgiving trip.

"That's it," he said when my arm went weak. Soon that layer was cleared as well.

That afternoon I took a long nap, one of the few I'd taken in my life, and awoke refreshed. Another positive outcome of my new road.

One day I received a call from Helen Thayer, an author and adventurer, who I'd met the summer before. At age fifty, she'd become the first woman to complete a solo journey to the magnetic North Pole. She'd survived no less than seven polar bear attacks, almost lost the dog Charlie who was her sole companion and protector, and was practically halted by an ice storm when just days from her goal. Now this was a brave woman who knew no bounds.

But where did her strength come from? I wondered. Her short, stocky frame didn't look like it gave her the agility to attempt such a daring feat. If she'd passed you on the street, you might never have suspected her avocation. But I could feel her vitality; I could hear it in her voice over the phone. Then I remembered her eyes. Yes, her strength came through her eyes. They were ablaze, having harnessed the power of her inner world. How I longed for a strength that true to fill me.

My attention turned back to our conversation in time to hear her say, "The storm was so bad, I didn't know if I would make it to the Pole or even to the end of the week. So I broke up my time into one-hour intervals and concentrated on making it just that far. *It was survival.*"

Yes, I smiled as I thought, it's one day, one moment, one step at a time for me, too, in this strange new world I'd found myself in.

Before each chiropractic treatment, I was asked to describe my top five symptoms. Were they better than last week or worse? By how much? There was a scale for these ratings and the answers went on my chart. I had to *feel* the answers, not *think* them—remedial training for adrenaline junkies, a "Feel & Do" exercise for the soul. Pain became an ally, a vehicle that carried important information. My senses became my guides.

It stupefied my friend Jessica that even as a lifelong athlete, I'd been so out of touch with my body. But I explained that I'd learned discipline above all else. In practice I'd built up my limits. During competition, I'd surpassed them. I'd overridden any pain that had had the audacity to come near me, as I'd pushed harder and harder to win.

"We were rewarded for ignoring our feelings, Jessica," I added. "Once I heard a football player from my high school shout, *'Tape it up, coach, I'm going back in.'* He had three broken bones . . . yet he still wanted to play. The sick thing was that I understood him perfectly."

Reconnecting with my feelings was now top of my list of things-to-do. It was no longer an indulgence; it was a matter of survival. Each day when I awoke, I would take a survey of my mental and physical capacities. How did I feel? Was I alert? Where did I ache? Before long, "feeling" became automatic and a daily pattern emerged.

First, my throat swelled, and my lymph nodes became tender.
Second, the muscles in my back swelled up with flu-like aches.
Third, I became weak and couldn't stand for more than a few minutes at a time.
Fourth, a cloud moved into my head, blocking my concentration and short-term memory.
Last, the "light" went out in my eyes and I had to lie down.

That month I gave up my computer. Imagine, the general manager of an electronics company working with no computer. But I didn't even need the chiropractor to test my strength, I could feel it myself: the computer drained me. So I had to let it go, at least for a bit. I had to admit that I couldn't use it effectively and be open to the possibility that that was fine for now.

The little yellow sticky notes that littered my car and home formed puzzle pieces for me:

CFS wants me to take a break from my routine with my family and friends.

CFS wants me to do a couple of small projects or one big one—*that's it.*

CFS wants me to open my mind further than I've ever opened it before.

CFS wants me to be more spontaneous, to plan less.

CFS wants me to exercise in smaller bites.

CFS wants me to work shorter hours and fewer days a week.

CFS wants me to be alone more.

CFS wants me to connect more deeply, with fewer people.

CFS wants to show me that I am my own best friend.

CFS wants me to understand my own needs.

CFS wants me to let it show me the way.

CFS wants me to be very gentle with myself.

Viewed like this, CFS wasn't all that bad.

the energy cup

The old Sally gave away energy by the bucketful, gallons and gallons each day. Where did my energy go? That's easy: to everyone around me. To thinking about the past. To worrying about the future. It went everywhere except where I needed it to be—*with me.*

Over time this giving-it-all-away habit caused a large hole to form in what I call my "energy cup." Virtually all of my energy escaped through this hole. I was left with just two drops and an illness called CFS. One drop supported my vital signs (I knew I wasn't going to die, even though I may have wanted to). The other was for discretionary use. And if I used the latter to do something that was aligned with the real me, a new drop or two would be added to my cup, sometimes more. If, however, I did something that was *against* my natural grain, I would lose all but a single drop of energy and be bedridden until the start of the next day.

A call from a dear friend created a positive energy gain.
A call from a not-so-dear friend caused a drip, drip, drip.
A box of childhood letters created a positive energy gain.
Memorabilia from my failed marriage caused a drip, drip, drip.
Thinking out of the box created a positive energy gain.
Closed-minded colleagues or clients caused a drip, drip, drip.

Since my energy supply was so low at the time, I could sense the movement of even one drop in or out of my cup. This was the surprise gift of my illness, a kind of spiritual truth serum, a finely-tuned energy meter that steered me toward the direction of my heart.

It was no wonder that the huge bags of vegetables and megadoses of vitamins that I'd taken the year before had had no lasting effect. Any energy they'd created had just fallen out of the big "hole" in my cup. I needed to plug the hole by learning how to manage my energy before any type of strength-building techniques could be long-lasting. Before my eyes could begin to sparkle with an inner fire.

Jessica caught right on. "A drip, drip, *gush* happens to me every time I go to the basement and see the boxes of my husband's books and notes from law school. Why does he keep these things, I ask you? You know he'll never look at them again. It drives me crazy!"

Over the next months, with my symptoms as my guide, my energy cup faithfully at my side, I systematically changed more than 1,000 things about my life. I felt my way through every duty, each person, thing, and activity. If a symptom flared or if my energy cup drained by even one drop, I'd get rid of whatever or whoever it was, no questions asked. If a wave of energy came into my cup, I'd keep it or them. Nothing was beyond scrutiny—not one piece of clothing, not one decision, not one relationship. It was survival.

And it wasn't easy. I was scared of changing so many things about my life. Scared to say yes to something new. Scared to say no to something I'd done for years. I plodded forward, day by day, drop by drop, one small step at a time, aligning my life with the real me.

As slow as it seemed at times, I must have been making real progress. One day my ex-husband stared right at me and had no idea who I was.

"Hi!" I shouted in surprise as he put his breakfast tray at the table right next to mine in the airport restaurant. He looked over, but his eyes didn't register knowing me. I couldn't believe it. We'd split up less than two years before.

"It's *Sally,"* I said.

"Oh . . . *hi,"* he said, his expression changing from a polite stare to a forced smile in the moment that the memory took hold. "You've . . . changed your hair."

"Sure," I replied, knowing that much more than my hair had changed since we'd last parted company. When he'd finished his food, said a polite good-bye, and taken a seat near his gate, I decided to walk over to where I could see him, but he couldn't see me. He was seated at the end of an aisle, reaching for a book. His movements were so familiar. I knew each one by heart. I could predict how his shoulder would shift as he turned his head, how his arm would move, even the expression on his face.

Okay, Sal, it's time, I said to myself. *Feel, girl, feel. You can do it.* My job was to breathe and let my feelings take care of themselves. The anger that had been the predominant feeling in our relationship came back, then left almost as quickly. A feeling of love lightened my heart. Pity, then sadness followed, punctuated by a final wave of guilt. The symphony of sensations was amazing. This "feeling" stuff wasn't so bad.

On the plane, I opened the *Hua Hu Ching*, the companion to the *Tao Te Ching*, that ancient Taoist philosophy book that had stirred my soul the year before. I flipped to a dog-eared page, poem No. 58, reading it for the fifth or sixth time. *"When the mind and spirit are forced into unnatural austerities or adherence to external dogmas, the body grows sick and weak and becomes a traitor to the whole being . . . ."*

Suddenly my body burst with sensations similar to ones I'd felt before, but less choppy and much better defined. There were memories of how I'd contorted myself to please, how I'd given up my soul to serve another's, and how my body had became exhausted in the process, both "sickening" and "tiring" me. The heaviness, the weight of society's rules. Bosses' demands. Parents' desires. What I was supposed to say and what I wasn't. Trying to please everyone else, while being so hard on myself. The illusion that *this* was what I needed for my survival.

"I've been as busy as a chameleon in a box of crayons," one of our board members used to joke. My body pulsed with a new understanding of those words.

When I returned to the office, I could feel how even our company had been contorting itself to please its customers. We'd tried to be everything to everyone. Using the anger that this stirred up in me as a fuel, I began to make changes to our business practices. We started to be very picky about the new customers we'd pursue. We'd only work with companies who were a sure-fire match with our technology, temperament, and tastes. Crazy, you say? Not at all. Our hit rate rose from winning one out of every fourteen contracts to landing two out of every three.

To my delight, a graceful flow had begun to build, lighting a spark within me, the individual team members, and the team as a whole. Our results were undeniable.

I was still taking my Wednesdays just for me. On one such Wednesday, I noticed a flyer from a local therapist and casually read the first few lines. It spoke of stress much the same way as the Taoist philosophy book did, as a gap between our inner world and outer skin—faking life in some small, but important way. My heart jumped. I'd found a modern-day Lao Tzu, someone who understood contortions and could help me dig my way out of mine. I called her immediately.

Before, I had thought of stress in terms of work deadlines and to-do lists. But through energy chiropractic and this lovely lady, I learned that my body stayed strong when I thought of the stress of a million-dollar negotiation, but was brought to its knees by seemingly trivial things—the thought of returning certain personal phone calls, for example.

"Find someone who loves you," Dr. Rapoport had told me nearly a year before. "You need to work with a therapist who really loves you." Boy was he right, and what a difference it made. From our very first appointment, the new therapist genuinely thought more of me than I thought of myself and stuck to this notion with more conviction than the best grandmother would (even an Italian one). She never wanted me to rush to an appointment, preferring that I'd come a few minutes late instead. After-hours phone calls were more than fine. Yes, I'd found the right support at last, someone who could stay a step ahead of me and complete every pass.

The therapist understood overachievers. "We *do,* therefore we have value," she'd say. "We secretly dream of a time when we'd be relaxed, at peace, and able to really rest." Her words were both invigorating and eerie, like she was reading my mind or had been spying on me during my first attempt at relaxation (that week of starting each morning with a nice cup of tea).

"Yes, relaxation can be quite difficult," the therapist would remind me. "Occasionally we can clearly see that life is here to enjoy, treasure, and cherish. But then this moment can pass just as quickly as it can come," she'd add, "leaving us to question if it had really been there at all. Confused, we then return to our rushed, frenetic lives, deciding that they're the ones we can really count on."

The chiropractor worked with my body as the therapist worked with my mind. Each week, I learned more about what filled and drained my "energy cup," and realized that this cup was my ticket to the real me. When I was faced with a decision, even a small one like what to have for dinner, I reached inside first. Would the choice give me energy or take it away? Did my symptoms flare or subside? Did I want to do it because I really, really wanted to or because I was afraid not to? Each answer illuminated my new world.

To lighten my load, fill my cup, and align with the real me:

- I moved from a house into an apartment.
- I sold my 1983 Toyota Tercel and bought an automatic-shift car with electronic everything.
- I pumped gas only at stations where they have auto-pay equipment and gas pump holders.

- I threw away my lists and did just what was on the top of my mind.
- I turned down invitations that I wasn't thrilled to accept.
- I said no to activities if I was tired, even if it meant going back on my former word.
- I gave up one very close friend.
- I hired a housekeeper.
- I mended all my clothes—skirts lined, buttons attached, and hems fixed.
- I cleared out my bookcase of all of the books I should have read but hadn't yet.
- I printed personal business cards and stationery.
- I bought wheeled luggage and carried less on-board an aircraft.
- I bought a larger size pair of jeans.
- I started dyeing my hair to get rid of the gray and freed the curls by letting them grow.
- I took a lesson in how to put on makeup.
- I gave up big photo albums in favor of "best of" albums with enlargements of only my very favorite shots.
- I did a cartwheel for the first time in fifteen years.
- I cooked a dinner of sautéed mushrooms.
- I took home the last of my childhood things from my parents' attic.
- I baked a birthday cake for an eleven-year-old friend so she could put her face in it—just for fun.

By the end of July, although my "five daily symptoms" were still with me, they had significantly lessened in intensity. More importantly, I was learning which small adjustments I could make to postpone their onset. I was able to take regular twenty- to thirty-minute walks, much better than the labored ten-minute walks of the spring. My sleep was still a struggle, but my nerves were calm. Jessica and I wondered if "healthy" people understood that there was such a physical (not just psychological) price to pay for keeping have-to's, should's, and clutter around.

Perhaps I could just step over the rough spots now and not let the thought of encountering a new one worry me. Maybe it was okay to let down my guard and relax a bit more, at least another magical half degree.

I started acupuncture treatments again, about a year after the initial round. Even on the first treatment, I sensed its effect on my body, a big contrast to the year before. The energy movement felt like a wave of happiness, an open, expansive flow. After each treatment my eyes would be bright. I'd smile, even occasionally glow.

One night I had a disturbing dream about the office. There was a fire smoldering in one of the back rooms, something that no one seemed to have noticed but me. I waited until after normal business hours to take the important files out to my car to protect them—secretly.

The therapist asked how I'd *felt* at each stage of the dream.

"Let's see," I said, closing my eyes to bring the memory back more clearly. "I felt scared. But when others were there, I hid the fact that I was scared. I acted like everything was fine. But when I was moving those files, the fear raced through my body . . . I literally *shook."* In the safety of her office, I let the terror of the dream fill me once again.

The therapist, prodding into an area that I suspected she already knew the answer to, asked if the fire had ever actually erupted.

"No," I replied, the feeling of terror instantly subsiding. "It never did, did it?"

The fire was a symbol of the 24/7 alert I'd trained myself to be under in my attempt to ward off danger and smooth over any rough spots in my day. Perhaps I could just step over the rough spots now and not let the thought of encountering a new one worry me. Maybe it was okay to let down my guard and relax a bit more, at least another magical half degree.

One teeny tiny step at a time, I was discovering the contents of the backpack that I'd been carrying, the heaviness that had caused me to become so chronically fatigued that my body broke down under its weight. And since the western doctors didn't have an operation or pill that could cure my illness, it was my hope that my newfound lightness would eventually alter the chemistry of my body, and that one day I'd make a full recovery.

On Monday, August 22, 1994, I had the first sign that I was right.

the turning point

My symptoms started a little after lunch. People came in and out of my office as usual. But something quite unusual happened that day. As I was awaiting the fog bank to roll into my head—symptom No. 4 on my daily list of five—a wave of energy swept through my body, lifting my weakness and sending my muscle aches away. I turned my head in disbelief, much as I'd done on the plane the day that CFS had first arrived, sensing that something strange was happening, and trying to figure out why. Sleep had been the only thing that had reset my symptoms in the past.

I put a big red star on my calendar. It was a very special day.

The next Wednesday I told my acupuncturist that I found it hard to sit still. It felt, quite literally, like I was crawling out of my skin. A few days later, I became aware of the skin over my entire body in a way that I'd never experienced before. It had come alive. *I* had come alive—at least temporarily.

Two weeks later, I pulled on my leotard and took a cautious look in the bedroom mirror. All I saw was lumps, and longed for the days that I'd had a tight, trim body. I fought back the urge to stay home and dragged myself to the dance studio for the first time in almost two years.

"It's so nice to see you again, Sally," chimed the dance instructor. "You look great. What have you been up to?" Her agile body moved close to mine, casting a delightful spell. Clearly her eye was not as critical as mine. To her my lumps were curves, the mark of a woman.

I made it halfway through the one-and-a-half hour class and was quite proud of myself, not only because of the exercise, but because I didn't force myself to stay until the end.

My concentration abilities were coming back, too. I decided to do some shopping.

"I'd like a laptop computer," I said, my heart filled with anticipation. "It has to be really light, have a brightly colored screen, and run the usual business programs. I don't care about the rest."

I was no longer an engineer. I was an artist.

On one of my Wednesdays I decided to try foot massage (reflexology). Don't ask me why. I just wanted to. Through the feet one can access all the muscles, organs, and glands, and rebalance the entire body.

"Hello," the reflexologist called out as I entered her office. "I'll be out in a few minutes. Just finishing up here." I could see her through the crack in the door, sitting on a stool at the end of a massage table. Her client's feet were bare, pants rolled up to just above his ankles.

"Have you ever had a reflexology treatment before?" she asked when she came out.

"Can't say that I have."

"Ooo, we're going to have a lot of fun then."

As she touched my feet, she sensed that my body was filled with toxins, then rubbed what she called the "liver area." I couldn't tell for sure, but I think that she was using a tool of some kind, or several different tools, perhaps. It hurt a little and it felt like there were chunks of hard crystals under my skin.

"And what are you so worried about?" she continued. "Your body has a high level of anxiety." I wasn't sure how to respond. Luckily, she broke the silence.

"People's emotions can get lodged in the different parts of their bodies and cause disease. Many people think that the two aren't related, but they are. One of the reasons I love my work so much is that I can help people release the emotions, which, in turn, helps the body relax. Have you ever noticed that the word disease is actually *dis-ease?*"

After the hour-long treatment, my feet rolled inward instead of out. I felt taller. My eyes were noticeably brighter. When I got home, I threw away my two favorite pairs of shoes. The pattern worn into them just didn't seem to fit my feet anymore. It was another step forward on the road that now seemed a little more mine.

Time was moving quickly now. Work was going along smoothly. An engineering manager from another division came to my office to tell me that it was refreshing for him to see that work could be fun, as well as productive. I took the compliment to heart.

My boss must have agreed, too, because when he decided to combine two of our divisions, he put me in charge of both. I accepted the assignment, even though the other division operated under a traditional business philosophy and was quite suspicious of our alternative approach.

As a first step, I gave the new 150-person group an "adjustment" to help our "spine" move with more flexibility and ease. The vehicle I used was a simple seating change. I broke up a cluster of negativity—four people who were at the center of the division gossip mill. With each now surrounded by positive people on all sides, one left the company, one transferred divisions, one blossomed, and one stayed the same. And more than one of the other team members made a special trip to my office to thank me for the change in atmosphere.

Then it was Jessica's turn to push me forward, to give me a front-end alignment of sorts. "You're better now, Sally. You really are," she said. "Can't you see it yourself? Are you ever going to stop all these treatments? You've got the chiropractor, the acupuncturist, now the reflexologist . . . and don't let me forget, the therapist, too."

My pulse quickened as if I were being attacked. "These treatments have saved my life, Jessica. I think they'll always be good for me."

"I think you're selling yourself short, Sally. Sure, they support you. They take away some stress. But you are also taking away stress with every single decision you make. Because you're making your own choices now, perhaps for the first time in your life, aligned with the real you. I've known you for a long time, Sally. I can see the change. Your new glow, the vitality you bring to your management style . . . these aren't from the supplements that you take or the massages that you get. It's from how you've aligned your life with who you really are, and brought fun to what the normal person would view as a heavy, demanding job. You run a twenty-four-hour-a-day *factory*, don't forget! When is CFS over, Sally? When can you call yourself cured?"

"You won't forget what you've learned," Jessica added, her tone turning gentle. "You're a new person now. It's time to act like one."

"I'm afraid if I say it out loud I'll jinx myself," I replied. "Even though my symptoms have gotten a lot better, they still flare up a little each day. I'm not sure when they'll disappear for good. Many people with CFS stay sick for decades."

I didn't want to say good-bye to my illness. I really didn't. My symptoms had guided and protected me more diligently and consistently than anyone ever had before. I appreciated them. I even loved them.

"You won't forget what you've learned," Jessica added, her tone turning gentle. "You're a new person now. It's time to act like one."

there's no place like home

As new seedlings were bursting through the spring ground, something began stirring within me, pushing the words that Dr. Rapoport had spoken almost two years before to the front of my mind, combining them with Jessica's.

Sally, put down your external priorities and toolbox of survival tactics. Put them down. You will not just survive anymore. You need to change your motivation from externally-based to internally-based, to one that is nurturing to you . . . Remove all external forces and discover who you are. Become a waitress if you need to. You need to learn how to feel, not do—to feel and own all parts of yourself.

Suddenly I realized that I'd actually learned the lessons that he'd set out before me that day. I could now feel . . . and feel the difference between choices made from the "inside out" versus those driven from the "outside in." And I now knew, because I'd experienced it, that by religiously serving my inside self, I could actually serve the outside world both more easily and better than I ever had before.

As my breath opened in celebration, a powerful insight chose that moment to arrive, aggressive in its mission, and tender in its approach. The insight had been teasing me for weeks, showing up in my chiropractor or therapist's offices, then hiding as soon as I'd step out the door. It revealed itself once in a conversation with Jessica, only to duck for cover as soon as I'd hung up the phone. I remember remembering there was something I'd wanted to remember, but couldn't remember exactly what that something was. Now, about three weeks after its first visit, the insight returned. I whipped out my pen and wrote it down.

Before the symptoms comes the wave. Before the wave comes the voice. If I follow the voice, I can ride the wave, and I don't need the symptoms anymore. When my body trusts me to follow the voice as consistently as I've followed the symptoms, I won't need the symptoms anymore.

My scribbles spoke of an inner voice, something that people often call intuition, but it was much more concrete and tangible than that to me. This voice spoke to me not with words, but through a knowingness, and always spoke just before energy dropped in or dripped out of my energy cup. It spoke the split-second before a symptom would flare. And there was no doubt about it, when I listened for this voice, it was always, always there. I could count on it to guide me, and more importantly, I could count on myself to listen. I didn't need the heavy hand of CFS anymore.

I felt like Dorothy after the fake wizard had been exposed. The answer had, indeed, been inside of me all along. Yes, I had the brains, heart, and courage to live a life that was truly alive. I'd always had these things. The only thing I'd ever lacked was an experience to draw these parts of me out, the friends at my side to support me, and a wise mentor or two—"good witches" who understood the big picture much better than I did myself. With that secret revealed and three simple clicks of my heels, I'd found home in no time at all.

step 1, feel

GOAL: COME BACK TO YOUR SENSES. *If you are anything like the "old Sally," living an efficiency-first and rules-oriented life according to the numbers, with a tight schedule and oh-so-ordered-and-focused-on-duty days, you run the risk of slowly cutting yourself off from the wonders of your true feeling nature. In this step we play with our five senses to awaken them, stir their juices, and bring us a little more alive.*

Webster's dictionary uses 233 words to define just one—"feeling." At their most basic level, our feelings are the urges in the body that alert us to go to the bathroom or get something to eat. They serve our fundamental need to survive. But they have a more complex side, too, one that adds a rich dimension to life, causing us to laugh at jokes, seek the sun to lighten our hearts and darken our skin, marvel at music, melt at a simple touch, come alive with *In their sweet, often myopic, and always persistent way, feelings are trying to help us.* fury, die of curiosity, reach for a drink, skip down a street, and jump headfirst into something new. We relax with pleasing feelings, cry with sad feelings, stuff down painful feelings, recoil at creepy feelings, and get embarrassed when a feeling we'd rather not reveal shows through anyway. Feelings surprise us with their intensity, confound us with their complexity, and, no doubt about it, bring humanity to life.

Feelings spring up to protect us from re-experiencing something that has been painful to us in the past. For example, if we've been hurt before by trusting someone who betrayed us, we'll usually feel cautious the next time we attempt to trust again. In their sweet, often myopic, and always persistent way, feelings are trying to help us. Though when they sing that same old tune one too many times, they hamper forward movement, as well as defy rational thought.

It's easy to throw up our hands at our feelings, but in this step it's finally our chance to lighten up and play with them instead. To begin our exploration, let's start with the basics, our five senses, those familiar surface sensations of sight, smell, hearing, taste, and touch.

Our skin helps us feel both the heat of a fire and the passion of a caress. Our taste buds sour at the tartness of a Granny Smith apple as well as the unpleasantness of an experience. Our ears get lost in the gentle rustling of a breeze in one instant, then in the next can pick out the cry of our child among all the other children in a playground. Our eyes allow us to see physical objects as well as tell when someone is lying to us. Our noses both smell the perfume of a flower and tell us if we'll like the thing we're about to eat. Our senses serve us on a practical level, and bring out the beauty of life.

We count on the physicality of our senses. We like to "see" something before we believe it. A "seer" predicts the future. We "foresee" events. When we've "heard" something more than once, it gets our attention. Something "smells a bit funny" to us when we don't think it's true. We "touch on" a new subject as we introduce it to someone for the first time. We "picture" things happening. We "see" it with our own eyes. Missouri is the "show me" state. Right now, you may be nodding your head in agreement, saying "I see" what we're talking about.

But the old expression "*Seeing is believing,*" actually started out as "*Seeing is believing, but feeling is the truth.*" Apparently Americans dropped the second half of the expression over the years as they dropped their reliance on the deeper use of their feeling natures.

Sure, feeling our feelings can mean that we may feel uncomfortable at times—but who cares? With a little practice, we can get comfortable with discomfort, as well. It's the groundwork we need for the rest of the book, where with each subsequent step we go deeper and deeper into ourselves. The more we are connected to what's going on under our skin, the more we understand what's right for us (and only us), and the better we can bring our unique perspectives to the world. Our attention shifts from the sticky surface sensations to the truer, cleaner, purer, and more powerful voices of our souls. And life takes on the fullness of a waterfall rather than the efficiency of chemically-treated water from the tap. New sensations and choices appear. Movement—of emotions, choices, habits, and energy—is what a soulful life is all about!

let the games begin: Now if you're ready, let's begin the games in our playground. Get out your favorite pencil, pen, or crayon. Use the margins to scribble in. Do any (or all) of the exercises that pique your interest in some way. And if you think you're the type of person who can't feel anything, simply pretend you can and begin.

1. basic feelings (*over the next 24 hours*): This may seem simple, but I'll bet that at least some of you will find it deceptively difficult. So many of us run our lives according to the demands of our family, our jobs, and our busy schedules, that we postpone even the most basic bodily needs. So for the next twenty-four hours, try honoring your body's desires, resisting the urge to put your routine ahead of yourself.

- **EAT WHEN YOU ARE HUNGRY AND ONLY WHEN YOU ARE HUNGRY.** If you're part of a family and have a fixed eating schedule, become more aware of how hungry you actually are (or aren't) at mealtime. Then adjust the amount you eat accordingly.
- **DRINK WHEN YOU ARE THIRSTY AND ONLY WHEN YOU ARE THIRSTY.** All the time.
- **GO TO THE BATHROOM EVERY SINGLE TIME YOU NEED TO.** Yes, this means don't hold it in if you can help it. Excuse yourself and do what your body needs you to do.
- **SIT DOWN, NAP, OR GO TO SLEEP WHEN YOU ARE TIRED.** Even sitting down for ten seconds will send the signal to your body that you're listening to its needs. Parents, this means you!

2. funny feelings *(a few seconds):* Do something a kid would do. Put your finger in your bellybutton and wiggle it around. Make your mouth into fish lips. Squeeze your right butt cheek, then your left, then keep it up until you're rocking back and forth. Wiggle your toes. Circle your arms like a windmill. Overachievers, do all these at once.

3. good memories *(2 minutes):* Following is something a friend sent to make me smile. Now I'd like to pass that smile on to you. It's a list of experiences, most of which you have likely had at one time or another. Don't just read them, don't just think about them, *feel* each of them. Hang out with each feeling for ten seconds or a full minute—more if you'd like. Let the feelings really, really fill you.

Move to a comfortable position and start.

- Falling in love for the first time
- Taking a hot shower
- Finding money in your newly-washed jeans
- Seeing the face of a delighted child
- Realizing it's an hour earlier than you thought
- Smelling chocolate chip cookies straight out of the oven
- Taking your first roller-coaster ride
- Getting into a freshly-made bed

4. bad memories *(5 seconds–5 minutes):* Do the memory exercise again, but this time with memories that you would rather avoid feeling. See if you can become as comfortable with the ebb and flow of negative feelings as with the more positive variety.

Move to a comfortable position and start. And remember to breathe.

- The loneliness after a break-up
- That phone call you were dreading
- Having the hot water run out during a shower
- Getting a huge credit card bill
- Realizing it's an hour later than you thought
- Having that pair of jeans not fit
- Finding something moldy in the fridge
- Really bad traffic

You may be feeling a little tensed up after reading this list. That's normal. If you'd like, scan the last exercise to relax and open yourself up once again.

5. body sensations *(1 minute each day for a week):* Finding today's day on the chart, list up to three physical sensations that your body has right now—perhaps a headache, a stomach pain,

body sensations						
monday	tuesday	wednesday	thursday	friday	saturday	sunday

a runny nose, a tension in your neck, a weird taste in your mouth, a tiredness in your eyes, a pitter patter in your heart, a gurgling in your tummy, or an ache in your shoulder. Avoid using broad words like "a cold" or "cancer." The sensations must relate to a physical part of your body, and how that part is feeling—and they don't necessarily have to be "bad."

Then when you wake up in the morning for each of the next six days, notice if these sensations are the same, better, worse, or if the feeling is gone. Record your answer in the appropriate box. If something new has sprung up, add it to the list and track it for the rest of the week. Notice how specific body sensations can change each and every day.

6. three energy centers *(3 minutes):* We have three basic energy centers that provide us different kinds of guidance: our head, heart, and gut. We can all relate to the kinds of advice our head gives us. It's logical, practical and, for the most part, sane. Our hearts are the gateways to our souls, containing our most delightful, often irrational, desires. Our gut is a wonderful balancing force, the rudder of our ship, so to speak. Its voice is like that of a straight-talking grandparent.

See if you can feel the three forces within you. As you are reading these words, move your attention to your forehead (putting your hand there will help). Feel what your mind is doing, if it's tired or crisp, and any thoughts it's having right now.

Then move your attention (and both hands) to your heart. Breathe into it a few times using the natural rhythm of your breath. Notice if you become more or less relaxed. Have your thoughts become more or less active? Has your breath moved any farther down in your chest?

Finally, as you read these words, move your awareness to your gut, placing your hands squarely on your belly as a guide. Breathe into this belly a few times using the natural rhythm of your breath. Notice if anything gurgles, flutters, or burps. Do you feel stronger or weaker than you did a moment ago? Less or more calm?

There are no right answers here, just the gentle opening that awareness brings. Don't be hard on yourself if you can't feel anything at all. It'll come.

7. changing pace *(2 minutes):* As you are experimenting with feeling, try adding some movement and see what happens. Either right now or the next time you get up, put on some comfortable shoes, a jacket perfect for the weather, and walk for precisely three minutes at precisely *half* the pace you're used to. Notice how you feel. Is it strange, fun, or both? Do you feel an anxiety building, wanting to get back to your normal pace? Are you noticing things about your neighborhood that you hadn't noticed before?

8. taste your food *(during your next meal, snack, or splurge . . . or right now):* For my Italian relatives, each meal is important—each bite of food, in fact. They can even tell if the broth for the risotto was made with bouillon or steeped on the stove from fresh vegetables. It's amazing.

During your next meal, snack, or splurge, don't chastise yourself for your choice of food or the pace at which you are eating it. Bring your attention to the particular taste or texture you were craving when you sat down to eat. Did you pick that particular food to be pleasing or just because it was quick? Is it satisfying you . . . or leaving you wanting something more? If you are rushing at all, slow down just enough to concentrate on the *taste* of the food, for a count of three. And if you are wolfing down a dozen donuts, it's perfectly fine to let the powder stay on your chin.

9. chew *(during this same meal, snack, or splurge . . . or right now):* Bring your awareness to the physical act of chewing. Notice the technique you use to chew your next bite of food. Do you leave the food partially whole as you swallow it . . . or let it dissolve completely in your mouth before sending it down the chute to your awaiting stomach? Just notice how you do it. Don't judge it. We're playing here.

10. feel your way *(5–10 minutes):* Take a spontaneous adventure in your own town, letting your feelings be your guide. It doesn't matter if you do it on foot, riding a bike, jogging, or in a car. Let your feelings tell you what turn to take next, which direction to move. Feel whether you want to turn right or left, go up the hill or down, turn into the alley, or through the field. My favorite time to do this is when I'm doing errands in the car. I'll make a turn I've never tried before and see where it leads.

11. first impressions *(2 minutes):* We dress up to make a better one, are told not to put too much faith in them, and kids and pets are great at them, sizing up people in one second flat. And aren't they usually right? Think about it—*firsts*. First kisses hold such power. That first brush of the skin. The first sightings of shore that have filled many a seaman's heart. As managers, we capitalize on first impressions that new employees have of our processes and possibilities. My cousin Patrizia won't read the same book or see the same movie twice. She cherishes the impact of that very first time.

Jot down the first impressions you had of the various people in your life. Were they right on the money or off? Any surprises arise? Overachievers, take the show on the road, pull up a seat at your favorite coffee spot, and spend five minutes collecting as many first impressions as you want.

12. day dream *(5 minutes):* Write down what would make you the happiest you can possibly be. The sky's the limit. Dream.

fill the page if you can.

keep going . . . fill that page!

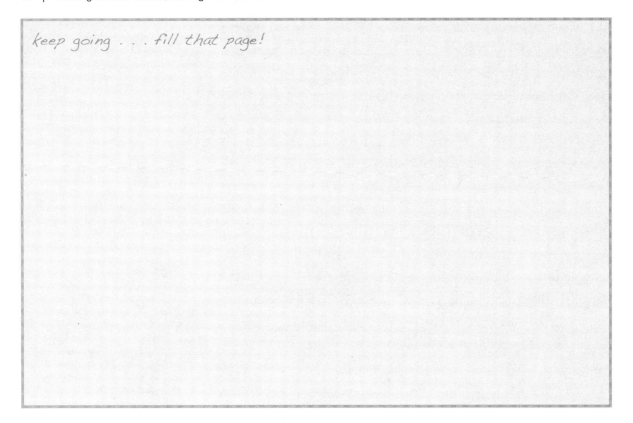

13. night dream *(5 minutes):* Sometime during this next week if you remember at least a fragment of a dream, no matter how big or small it is, write it out in as much detail as you can. Then go back over it one more time and add the feelings you had during each and every scene.

If you were talking on the phone in the dream, for example, did you like the person you were talking to or not? If there was a knock on your door, were you surprised or had you expected it? If your house was burning down in your dream, were you terrified or relieved? If you were flying, were you scared or delighted by your power?

Again, there is no need to interpret any symbols or feelings. Simply notice as much of the dream with as much precision as you can. We're just practicing.

14. dreams come true *(tonight):* Go to sleep one hour before your normal bedtime. See how that feels. Overachievers, go to bed two hours before you usually do. If you can't actually fall asleep, take the time to read, rest, and generally relax until you drift off to dreamland.

wrap-up

Have you ever noticed that four out of our five senses are located in the head? No wonder our attention is so often drawn above our necks. With our senses so abundant there, it's natural for us to retreat to our brains and get lost in thought, worries, or plans.

But consider for a moment that our skin is our largest organ, holding our fifth sense, touch. Our sense of touch is vital to us: babies can literally die without it and even the most powerful adult can melt into a blubbering fool under its power.

We have surface sensations of sight, smell, hearing, taste, and touch. Then deeper down, under the skin, behind the breasts, bellies, and belly buttons, we find our organs—things we don't normally associate with our senses, but that are connected to them just the same. The lungs that draw in our breath, that tighten as we worry, and that can stop altogether when we're really, really excited or really, really afraid. There's a heart that holds our capacity to love. A gut that can both wrench with uncertainty and, like a battleship, propel us decisively forward. And underneath everything, through the gateway of the open heart, is the soul, a vast ocean within, the main subject of Dive (Step 5) and the underlying force behind this whole book. We are so much more than our achievements, duties, and dreams.

step 2, clean

GOAL: **CLEAN OFF WHO YOU AREN'T.** *This step is a lightening, a lifting, a judicious and delicious use of the word "no." We "feel into" (rather than "look at") the people, activities, and stuff of our everyday lives to see where the heaviness is located and how to lighten it up. Yes, some of the decisions we make will be hard. But that's because they will be changes to the way we normally do things, steps into something new.*

Life normally doesn't come with guarantees, but this book has one for you. I guarantee that by the time you finish reading it, you will have more energy than you do right now. The bulk of the initial work, in fact, is to get rid of where you are wasting your energy, both physically and emotionally. In order to become light enough to soar with your soul, initially, some *dis*assembly is required. That's what this step is all about.

Imagine how our souls feel when they are lost in the chaos in our lives—the woulds, coulds, and shoulds that drive the choices we make, giving priority to the needs of the outside world at the expense of our own. When our souls get scared or go into hiding, we lose touch with both our inner selves and our big picture perspective. Slowly and surely we turn to society's rules to make our choices, labeling this "living," and pretending we are truly alive. We convince ourselves that it's an acceptable solution, often not remembering that an alternative even exists. Within this box, we feel safe, secure, and in control.

Our goal is to scratch beyond the surface layer and uncover areas where our daily activities aren't quite in alignment with who we really are, to notice where we feel an inner push-pull, the tug of an urge that's trying to fight its way up and out.

That is, until something happens that causes us to rethink the way we're approaching life. With the experience of opening to a new perspective—even a magical half degree—our pot of gold is found, pilot light lit. My flame began to burn on January 2, 1994, when I realized that my illness was meant to be my teacher, not my enemy. Everything changed right then and there. Mustering up what energy I had, I followed my body's lead, putting the attention on my feeling nature that I'd previously given to fighting my disease. It was the flip of a switch—on one hand, a huge deal. But on the other, so obvious that I felt silly that getting there had taken so very long.

In Feel (Step 1) we play with our five senses, feel our skin, gums, bumps, bulges, and tongues, and we open our taste buds, eyes, ears, minds, and lungs. Now, in Step 2, we dig deeper. Our goal is to scratch beyond the surface layer and uncover areas where our daily activities aren't quite in alignment with who we really are, to notice where we feel an inner push-pull, the tug of an urge that's trying to fight its way up and out.

It is within this paradox, the variety of sensations that go with our every move, that our humanness lives. The fears that can accompany failure and the ones that can push away success. The discomfort that we sometimes have with comfort, the stressful side of relaxation. The emptiness at the moment of a long-fought-for achievement. The urge to create and the urge to control, box-in, or make more acceptable this very creativity. The way we laugh until we cry.

When I first got ill, for example, a terror filled me. I was panicked by the immediacy and irreversibility of the change. But underneath those outer feelings was a small, lone voice. When it dared to speak, it would come forth and whisper its secret into my ear, telling me how relieved it was to be so very ill, to have a socially acceptable reason to say no to the outside world and finally have the chance to scream a huge, "*Yes!*" from the rooftops, a "*Yes!*" meant just for me.

But every time this feeling would arise, I'd chase it away, stuff it back down, afraid that someone else might hear it, embarrassed that it had appealed to me so much, even for a moment—feeling guilty, weak, and wrong to have listened to this voice at all.

In this step I'm asking you to do as I now say, not as I did then. Be kind to the little voice inside of you and listen to it when it speaks. You see, I learned the hard way that resisting it, prolonging the push-pull struggle, simply does not work. A push-pull always happens at the start of something new. It's natural. And the most powerful, equally natural, way to handle this feeling is to concentrate on the fire that's being stoked, on where it wants you to go, rather than cling to the old habits and routines as I did.

In this step we dive into our internal paradoxes, open up Pandora's box, and delight in the discovery that, even after all of those nasty emotions are unleashed, there remains a "hope" waiting patiently inside. We take a nice long feel (notice I didn't say "look?") into what brings energy to us and what drains it out. We relax a little (and laugh a lot) as we examine the activities, people, and stuff that fill up our lives. We open our perspective, casting out our worries about saying no to the world and saying yes to ourselves. And then we smile to ourselves when, a moment after the yes choice has been made, the "But should I really?" push-pull struggle begins.

A push-pull comes with every significant choice we make. But in this chapter we're going to experiment with *embracing* our urges instead of fighting them. We'll practice unwinding those springs, relaxing those curls, straightening out those knots, and pruning those bushes so their limbs have room to breathe from the *inside out.* The first step is to identify where there's an inner urge or energy drain that we're ignoring, fighting . . . or simply haven't noticed yet. Then we'll make our choices. And as I said before, it will take some work but no more energy than we are spending right now.

Feeling into my gut, where the energy cup is housed, I asked myself the same question dozens of times a day: is what I'm about to say, do, or think going to give me energy or take it away?

Most people think this step is great fun, giving them permission to make their needs important in a nonselfish way. But it can also feel like the slap that a prize fighter receives to revive him or the painful truth spoken from the lips of a good friend. Whether it feels good or bad to you, just remember that you keep more energy in your body when you align your external choices with your internal world.

To help us, let's invite three friends along—the energy cup that's built into each of us, an engineering concept called the signal-to-noise ratio, and a little taste of Italy.

the energy cup

You'll recall from my personal story that I discovered a built-in energy meter, an internal device that would tell me what was good for the real, authentic, unique me and what was not. A rush of energy would accompany things that were good for me, filling my energy cup. And I would lose energy even thinking about things that were not. When I was most weak with Chronic Fatigue Syndrome, I could feel when one drop came or went, a surprise gift when I began to look at it that way.

Feeling into my gut, where the energy cup is housed, I asked myself the same question dozens of times a day: is what I'm about to say, do, or think going to give me energy or take it away? My energy cup told me the answer. It felt like a blast of energy in . . . or a drip, drip, *gush* out. Then it was up to me whether or not to follow its advice. The effect of every decision I made was amplified in my weakened state, training me well, leading me ever so gently into a formerly unknown area, the trueness of my feeling nature and the desires of my heart. When I used my energy cup well, I made it through the day . . . when I didn't, I was forced back to bed to think about my choices.

We all have an energy cup. It helps us make decisions, like who to hang out with or what job to accept, bringing its own kind of logic to guide us through life's sweet and sticky spots.

broken energy cup?

time to sing the blues

One crisp fall day I was merrily skipping along, following my internal energy cup, my signal squarely at my side. A man popped up out of nowhere, the first potential date I'd met in a year. A rush of sweet energy filled me. Every body signal that I'd learned to count on was ringing its bell. For two days before our date I pranced around in happy expectation.

I circled the blues club until I found the perfect parking spot. After a final check of my make-up in the rear view mirror, I went in. But as soon as I saw him, sitting alone at a table sipping a microbrewery beer, I realized that I'd made a mistake. He was a nice man, but not the right one for me. I was crushed. How could my energy cup have lied? It had been sending me such strong signals and had never let me down before.

It took me a full week to figure out what went wrong. The pre-date feeling I'd had was not an intuitive truth, a heart's desire—it had been a craving. I'd been locked in a habit of looking for someone who *needed* me, rather than a person to enjoy and love. When I'd said yes to the date, it was my craving for being needed that was speaking so loudly, sending me all of those positive signals. My craving was masking my heart.

I felt into my body to see if I could sense the difference between my heart's true desire and my cravings. It took several days, but the answer came. My inner voice spoke straight from my gut. It was direct, simple, and strikingly clear. I actually felt lighter after having a true insight. When I had a craving, by contrast, I found that I literally salivated, as it lured me with its hollow promises, glamour, and panache.

I was proud that I'd trusted my second first impression and didn't agree to another date just to be sure.

the signal-to-noise ratio

Our second main tool is straight from the electrical engineering lab: the signal-to-noise ratio. Now don't get nervous, it's actually quite easy to understand. It's the measure of useless noise as compared to the signal that carries the important information. In designing an electrical circuit, engineers want the signal to be free from noise so that it has the most integrity. If the noise floor is too high, it can mask the signal entirely—like having static when you're listening to the radio. Perfection would be a strong signal in a sea of tranquility.

At my old company, we used the signal-to-noise ratio frequently. The spirit of our company, I told our engineers when I introduced the concept, was like the signal of an electrical circuit. Our distractions, the noise. A high ratio of one to the other ensures that our signal can be seen above the noise. It gives us a clear corporate focus and a distinct voice in the marketplace. Next, I drew a figure on the conference room board, a squiggly line across the top of a graph. The team recognized it immediately as a signal-to-noise ratio of 1:1. The signal was indistinguishable from the noise.

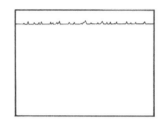

Then I drew another graph with the signal standing strong in the center and the noise floor bowing at its feet. "Now, pretend these are two companies. Which of them would you rather work for?"

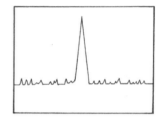

Chortles filled the room, and we began to toss ideas back and forth. We talked about how engineers use filters to reduce noise, amplifiers to boost signals, and how we might apply these same ideas to management. We discussed the animosity that two groups within our division felt for each other, and how this distracted our movements and added to our noise. Then we searched for one united vision, something that could motivate the whole team. We wanted our signal to stand out like Mount Rainier against the Washington landscape—solid, tall, and proud, with every subtlety revealed.

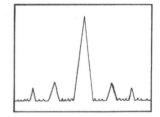

Now, let's look at the signal-to-noise ratio from a human perspective. A bad ratio is when your signal is being drowned out by the noise around it. Like trying to find a friend in a crowded theater. Talking to someone in a noisy restaurant. The kids screaming so loudly that you can't hear yourself think. Or when you are so focused on someone else's goals that you lose connection with your own.

It takes a tremendous amount of energy to navigate through clutter, distractions, and noise. Some people find it stimulating. Others comfort themselves with it. I find it at best aggravating, preferring to crawl out of my skin instead.

a taste of italy

The Italians seem to understand intuitively that each person has a voice, a signal to call their own. And as if paying homage to this, they do something that would make many Americans cringe. They force their youth at the tender age of thirteen to make a critical decision that will impact their choice of long-term career. Appalling, constricting, and wrong. Right?

Or could it just be a different way of looking at things— a more natural way, in fact? A realization that people are born with innate interests and inclinations, a foundation on which their lives should be built. It's already obvious by someone's early teens, readily visible and much less likely to have expectations distorting it or painful experiences piled on top of it, hiding them from who they really are.

At age thirteen, Italian youths choose which *scuola superiore* (high school) they will attend—*scientifico, linguistico, classico, tecnico,* to name a few—and this sets them on a certain track. From the science program one typically continues to become an architect, engineer, or doctor, for example. From the language program, international business or translator are common careers. From the broader liberal arts program, one could go into architecture or science, for example, or become a teacher, historian, or something else in this vein.

Italian kids are expected to know themselves, their most basic interests, well enough at age thirteen to choose which road is right for them. As funny as this may sound to an American, the Italians may very well be right. Perhaps as a culture they pay more attention to the early indication of signals taking life . . . and tend to each signal's growth well with Italy's slower, more sensitive pace.

let the games begin: Let's find those signals in the noise and discover more about our real selves. If you prefer the image of digging sand on a beach, put on your imaginary bathing suit and grab a plastic pail and shovel. Or if you're the more serious type, go get your archeologist's outfit and technical gear. It's time to play.

1. disappoint someone *(an instant):* We're going to get this one out of the way first, tackling the number one reason people keep extra stuff around: the fear of disappointing someone else. So disappoint someone—*as soon as you possibly can.* Find one promise you've made, one small thing that people count on you to do, that you've always done, or that perhaps you never considered not doing before, and just *don't* do it. It could be something tangible like mowing the lawn, always being the one to volunteer, or attending Sunday dinner. Or it could be a simple gesture like the perky expression you put on your face when someone asks you to do something. Whatever it is, the thing you pick must be something that, if you take the time to notice, feels a bit fake to you—even if it started out as invigorating and natural. It's a "should" rather than a joy, one of those borderline duties that's a habit, not a necessity. Find one small thing, and just *don't* do it. See how it feels.

2. sign on fridge *(2 minutes):* Make a sign for your fridge. Make up your own or choose from some of my favorites. The first one is from my friend Aurora.

- **THINGS TO DO TODAY:** *breathe out, breathe in, breathe out, breathe in, breathe out. . .*
- **RELAX, YOU DESERVE IT!**
- **LIGHTEN UP!**
- **I'M COMING TO MY SENSES!**

3. breathe *(1 minute):* As you are reading this, and without trying to force things one way or another, breathe in, and count how long it takes you to naturally inhale. Then count the exhale, too. Notice which is naturally longer for you, the inhale or the exhale . . . or are they the same? If you want, do it again. You have plenty of breaths to choose from.

Now bring your attention to the rest of your body. During an inhale, what happens? Does your chest expand? Does the breath go all the way to your belly or stay up higher? Can you get an in-breath to reach all the way down to your toes? Wiggle them and see if you can fill them with your breath's fresh energy.

Notice how long you play this game before your mood changes, one way or the other.

4. relaxation, part one *(5 minutes):* If you're like my friend Michelle, mother of four who found she'd been so busy for so long that she'd forgotten how to relax altogether, take this opportunity to jot down a few ideas of things that would feel really, really relaxing to you. Fill a full page as fast as you can to prime the pump and start the flow of your inner glow.

how i relax . . .

fill that page!

5. relaxation, part two *(2 minutes):* Think about the last time you were relaxed, really relaxed (if ever!). It could have been this morning or ten years ago. Or if you can't think of something specific, just imagine a general feeling of relaxation. That's right, with one breath, just breathe relaxation right in. With your next three breaths, fan this relaxed feeling into a nice roaring fire. Now to my favorite part: let this warm relaxed feeling slide down your tight washboard, soft, or pregnant belly, laughing its way through . . . down your thighs and calves, that movement-oriented part of you . . . . then, finally, to your toes. Wiggle them to be sure. Overachievers, fill your entire being with a relaxed sensation in one simple movement.

6. pretend you're a kid again *(3 minutes):* Can you remember back? What were your natural inclinations, the people, activities, and things you gravitated to? What we're after in this game is to think back to a life direction that had been with us from the start and may or may not still be with us now. It's not to say we all had them, we didn't. But if we did, bringing back the memory can be illuminating.

I wanted to be a ballerina, to use my body and my grace, to be a girly-girl. I was writing poetry at age eight, but in high school decided to be more practical and become an engineer. At age twelve, my Italian friend Teresa started tutoring students (and still continues to this day, some fifty years later).

What were your earliest inclinations? Are they still with you today?

7. three energy centers *(3 minutes):* Let's go back to the three energy centers that we introduced in Feel (Step 1)—our head, heart, and gut—and see what they're saying right now.

As you are reading these words, bring your attention to your head. How does it feel? Notice any comfort or discomfort, any tension or ease. Feel your head's logical nature, its practical side, its ability to break down large tasks into small, do-able steps. Imagine a series of gears turning around that facilitate your brain's movement.

Next, take a few seconds as you read these words to pull your thoughts from that big, beautiful brain, down your neck into that warm lovely heart of yours. Bringing your hands there will help. Rest both your hands and your full attention on your heart for a moment or two.

For some of us finding our hearts may feel quite strange, our attention will swim around and we'll be a little shaky, maybe wavering, running from corner to corner trying to locate the object of our desire. Others of us will feel absolutely nothing at all and return up to the brain to figure out what's going on. And those of us who have spent time in Italy, where hearts rule, will wonder what all the fuss is about, the answer is obvious to them.

Just notice how you feel with your hands on your heart, knowing that however you feel in this moment is just fine.

Now with your attention still on your heart (or in that general area), notice how your chest expands with your next inhale. Linger for a moment or two as your lungs fill up with air, then empty themselves once again. Overachievers, divide your attention between your chest and mind, then return your full attention to your heart center, and breathe in and out once again.

Everyone, bring both of your hands down to your guts, putting them over the fullest, flabbiest, or firmest part of your belly. Draw your attention inward to your center as you take three natural breaths. Then with your next breath or two, see if one word that describes you pops up from your gut to your mind.

Once again, there are no right answers to this game. The whole point is to strengthen our rapport with our bodies so we can better listen to what they have to say.

8. some disassembly required (*as many minutes, hours, or days as you want):* Here's my favorite part of this step—going through both our physical and invisible worlds to find the distractions, energy sinks, clutter, and fluff. Let's start with the physical first, then get more conceptual.

physical cleaning

The object of this game is to discover what drains you, what's putting a hole in your energy cup. Reach into your gut and locate your energy cup, the thing that tells you what gives you energy and what takes your precious energy away, what's "signal" and what's "noise" to you. Then plug the holes, get rid of the noise, and your signal will naturally rise. No searching for yourself is required.

note
this is a long exercise, divided into two parts (physical and invisible cleaning)

- **GO THROUGH YOUR HOUSE.** Go through your room, house, or apartment and get rid of anything and everything that drains your energy. If it bugs you at all, it has to go—even if no replacement is immediately available. Perhaps it's not logical at all, you just hate that outfit. Or it may look good on you, but it also reminds you how you starved yourself to squeeze into it. Photos of old boyfriends or girlfriends. Gifts that you're keeping to not offend someone. If they give you energy, great. But if they drain you or put the slightest extra burden on you, they have to go. The goal is to love every single thing in your home.

  There is an important difference between this game and a "less is more" simplicity mindset. The only rules in our game come from *within you.* If you love lipstick, t-shirts, or paint and having two cabinets filled with various colors brings you a rush of creative juice, by all means keep them. You win. But if those very same cabinets remind you of how you blow your budget and change your mind all the time, you'll feel your energy sink. Follow your energy and your decisions will be clear. Feel your way.

- **GO THROUGH YOUR CALENDAR.** Now grab that calendar that shows what you do in a week, and then be as ruthless with your activities as you were with your physical stuff. Are there any activities that you'd rather not do? Can you skip a party that you dread going to? Are you exhausting yourself playing chauffeur to the kids? Is the opera out, and a movie in? If it drains you to go to the gym, can you substitute a walk in a park instead? I mention these alternatives to stimulate your thinking. The important part of this game is not to find a substitute activity, it's to locate the biggest energy drains of your average week and get rid of at least one right away.

- **GO THROUGH YOUR ADDRESS BOOK.** People can be the biggest energy gains and drains of all. A long walk with one friend can be a delight, but two minutes with another can end up in a fight. Take as much time as you'd like to look through your friends, associates, and colleagues. Identify the ones who most drain your energy. Once, when playing this game, an advertising executive even got rid of some of her clients!

invisible cleaning

Let's clean up the world that we can't see or touch—the things we say, the heaviness we feel. Let's lift invisible weight off our shoulders.

- **WHENEVER YOU HEAR A COMPLAINT COMING OFF YOUR LIPS,** look to see if you are wasting energy, making life harder than it has to be, and adding to your noise. A woman told me that her mother has complained three times a day for a good forty or fifty years that she can never find her kids' phone numbers, while in a half hour's time one could easily have compiled a list. A small fraction of the energy spent complaining could be redirected to lifting the weight and solving the problem.

  What do you complain about? If your toddlers always want to play with your keys, why not make them their own set? If your cat likes to sleep on your nice wool sweater, why not get her one of her own from the nearest thrift shop? If it's a project that never quite gets done, why don't you admit you'll never do it, and cross it off your list. Think emotional lightness and energy savings, and follow your energy cup.

- **WHENEVER YOU KEEP A SECRET (OR WHITE LIE),** you know the kind I mean, it creates noise and uses energy, forcing you to remember who knows what about whom. Or when another person tells you a secret that you're supposed to keep track of, it's like putting an extra book in your bag to carry around all day. Enough! Are there any secrets that come to mind that you can just let out?

- **WHENEVER A DUTY FEELS HEAVY,** reposition yourself to see its bright side, the reason you're doing it, or the long-term goal. When a physical task can't be crossed off the list, your only choice is which attitude you put with it. Think about the duties you can't ignore, discard, or tell to go away, such as bills, family responsibilities, and jobs. Which is your heaviest? Is there a fresh attitude you can adopt that can make this duty feel lighter?

  Once I met two women who were both in the same difficult situation: each had an autistic child. Both of them worked outside the home. Both of them were dedicated mothers. But one felt weighed down, while the other lit up every time she talked about her son, clearly enjoying discovering how he learned, active in developing new teaching methods. Two women with the same issue, the main thing separating them being their attitude. One's cup was half-empty, heavy, laced with guilt . . . the other's half-full, open with curiosity.

- **WHENEVER YOU MAKE A PROMISE THAT ISN'T KEPT,** you are throwing a bit of your energy out of your cup (and perhaps putting a slow leak in someone else's). Did you keep the last promise that you made?

invisible weight loss

a personal reflection

Before I was ten, I had already given myself the job of family mediator. My antennae were on 24/7, alert for early signs of trouble. My words were precisely chosen for my role as each parent's interpreter. It was not a conscious choice on my part, just a thing that kids step up and do. As far as I was concerned, it was perfectly normal. But in my late twenties, ten years after I'd left home, an anger began to build inside me, a tension I couldn't ignore. I felt like I was about to burst, so I saw a counselor about it. Actually not about "it," exactly, but about my failing marriage. It's just that all of my conversations with the therapist eventually led to "it," the deeper turmoil that was sending my cork sky-high. Being a man of few words, a professional listener, the therapist offered but one simple comment.

"It seems like you think you're responsible for your parents' happiness, even today. Your parents are perfectly capable of finding happiness on their own. Do you realize that it's not your job?"

I was confused by his statements and found myself arguing with him. I pulled as many old memories as I could into my mind, searching for evidence to support my perception. But no matter how many scenes I flipped through in my mind's eye, I couldn't find *one single day* when I hadn't been worried about my family's happiness and that I hadn't searched for a way to help.

I left his office shaken and confused, my very foundation having been challenged to its core.

By the time I reached my house, his words had sunk in. It wasn't my job alone to keep the family harmony. My parents were competent. And others could help, too, and actually had. The bubble of tension inside me burst, the illusion of a lifetime revealed. I wasn't alone anymore with a burden, I now saw myself as one small part of a united team.

As I got out of the car, a huge weight lifted off my shoulders. It felt *physical,* not a mere metaphor—and several tons worth. I'll never forget the sensation, that split-second moment, the internal insight that had changed the way I viewed my outer world.

A few minutes later as I stood at the bathroom mirror, for the first time in my life I saw myself as beautiful, really beautiful. Before, I'd seen only my flaws, the woman who wasn't able to single-handedly make our household into a 1950s-ideal. With that absurdity gone, the inner beauty that others had always seen in me was free to shine through to my eyes.

I had but one short glimpse of my real self that day. My reflection turned back to its former state, awaiting a day when my inner beauty would come out for good. And as more of my invisible weights lifted, it did.

9. spontaneous body scan *(1 minute):* As you are reading these words, freeze your body position exactly where it is right now. Linger there for a moment or two, feeling where your head is positioned, then down the full length of your torso, legs, and arms. Next, relax as much as you can *in the exact same position you are in.* Find the most comfort you can, even in the face of discomfort.

10. survival modes *(2 minutes):* Let's examine the favorite survival modes we use when we're afraid or angry. Are you the type of person who *fights, flees,* or *becomes paralyzed?* Do you fight your way through something, run away from trouble, or sit there like a deer in the headlights . . . or sometimes try all three? Myself, I'm a fighter. Give me a mountain and I'll climb right up, something every boss I've ever had has loved (the irony being that I can often miss the easier paths to the same spot!).

When you identify your basic instinct, write down its main strength and weakness. Again, there's no right or wrong answer here, just a playful understanding of your unique way of doing things.

11. secret pockets of noise *(3 minutes):* These are the things that have been filling your head for so long that you may think they are universal truths. Circle the ones that ring even the least bit true to you. Overachievers, identify some thoughts of your own that are quite possibly limiting you.

- Work has to be hard.
- If something good happens, something else will happen to spoil it.
- I'm faking it. Soon someone will discover this and I'll be exposed.

- I'm not worth it. It's my family/career/_____ that counts.
- If I don't sacrifice myself, I'm not being a good parent/child/employee/role model/citizen/_____.
- I have to fit in. Being different is painful, even dangerous.
- I can't think about my own needs; I have too many responsibilities that take priority.
- Happiness is for the young.
- As I age, I'll lose energy and zest for life.
- There are never enough hours in the day.
- I'm always exhausted when I go to bed.
- I can't afford a real vacation.
- I don't have time to sleep the number of hours my body wants.
- Given my schedule, it's impossible to maintain a healthy diet.
- I'll never have enough money to make me feel really comfortable.
- I really don't have a choice. I have to do it/stay put.
- I could never live somewhere more peaceful.
- _____(fill in your own).

As an ending to this game, I want to plant one lovely thought in that big beautiful brain of yours. None of the statements has to remain 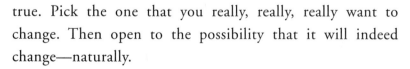 true. Pick the one that you really, really, really want to change. Then open to the possibility that it will indeed change—naturally.

12. the vice squad *(3 minutes):* I talked to my doctor about sugar cravings, one of my favorite foibles. "If it's malted milk balls you like," he said, "just how many do you eat? A warehouse-store-sized bag or just a few?" The directness of his question embarrassed me. I pictured myself in a room filled with malted milk balls, literally swimming in them. It made the handfuls that I'd eaten seem like a much less dramatic thing.

Let's look at the various ways we comfort ourselves—particularly the unconscious or exaggerated ways (like eating a whole gallon of ice cream when a mere pint would do!). The more we poke and prod at our absurdities, the easier it is to jiggle them loose, loosening their hold over us, letting our movements be more free. Creating choice is the name of our game, choosing anew from the inside out.

No matter how old, successful, or secure we are, we all need a little comforting at times. A well-placed compliment can brighten an entire day. The warmth of a hug can make even the craziest fears melt away. We reach for chocolate, the TV remote, books, beer, wine, or, unfortunately, drugs. Some of us exercise to get rid of tension, others turn to shopping or sex. People find comfort in their families, their children, and their pets. Others need external validation, counselors, compliments, or a caress. Many turn to work to satisfy themselves, to give them an outlet to run at full speed. Others prefer a natural tranquilizer and go out to the garden to weed.

What are your favorite ways to be comforted when you're feeling a bit down, bored, lonely, or upset? What are your favorite ways to comfort someone else?

My cat Zsa Zsa throws herself on the floor in front of me, rolls on her back so her big belly faces up, and insists that I pet her before I take another step. Overachievers, sometime today, be just as direct.

13. break suction *(1 week):* Cancel every single thing you possibly can, even the things you like to do or consider obligations, *for an entire week.* No complaints now, no grumbling. If you were sick or on a business trip you'd have to, so I know you can do it. But do it right now, just for you, directly. Create an extraordinary amount of free time this very week. Notice how light (or odd!) it makes you feel. Then pay particular attention to any new ideas, activities, or opportunities that come your way, enticed by the opening you've created.

wrap-up

Tell me, did this step do its job? Do you feel lighter than when you started? Do you have more permission to be yourself and know a little more about what being yourself really means? I go back to this step whenever I'm stuck or when I feel a bit heavy around the edges. I like its tangibility.

I've found that men, in particular, enjoy the signal-to-noise ratio as a reminder of the big picture we both unfold into and pull ourselves out of. The trick to using it, as with everything in this book, is to *feel* your way, to let your feeling nature join forces with the big, beautiful logic of your brain.

Feel free to tuck the energy cup and signal-to-noise ratio in your pocket or pin them up on your fridge. They enjoy being used. In fact, the more you tune in to these inner instruments, the more sensitive and astute they will become. Clean off who you aren't to let who you really are naturally rise up to greet you in the mirror and shine its unique perspective on the world.

step 3, polish

GOAL: SHINE UP WHO YOU ARE. *In this step we shift from eliminating the noise—the push-pulls, energy drains, and clutter—to directly feeling our signals. We identify what we know about ourselves and the gifts we bring to our outside world, paying particular attention to the people we connect with, and why. Then we discover where it's absolutely, positively, the easiest thing in the world for us to shine.*

stepping out

It's so tempting for activity lovers, doer-bees like me, to stay forever in the instant satisfaction of Clean (Step 2). We roll up our sleeves, clean up our lives, align our energies, and revel in freshness. There's plenty to do, clutter to clear, closets to clean, conversations to complete, and unspoken words to get out of the air. But alas, it's time to take the next step. Our floors are sparkling well enough, the dust bunnies are under control, our disassembly is done. It's time to give our signals the direct attention they deserve. Let's take a shower, put on fun outfits, and get those newly uncovered selves out into the world. Let's polish our shine.

Isn't it wonderful that just the act of getting rid of who we *aren't* will naturally bring out who we really are? When we

uncover our signals from the noise (our metaphor from Step 2), more of our truer selves shine through, free from their burden and weight. Yes, it *is* that simple.

Shining is just one quick flip of perspective. Once you feel satisfied that you're light enough, that you've cleaned up enough, simply refocus your vision, and look at what you have left. It may be all of you that you see or, more likely, it's just a portion of you, the tip of your signal peeking through what noise is still surrounding it. You may be tempted to go back and clean up some more, but now is the time to call enough enough, get out in the world, and polish your shine into a full-fledged glow.

The only thing to watch out for when we begin to strut our stuff is any of the newly exposed parts of our signals that may feel a little naked, raw, and sensitive to the light. We have to "unknow" ourselves, letting our outer selves catch up with the inner changes, and asking the people in our lives to do the same. That's the push-pull aspect of this chapter, the soul's dance as it blossoms inside of us, breaking itself free from its old routine.

When we unbury new aspects of ourselves, at times we rejoice in the fresh air we can breathe. But at other times we want to act out, to yell and scream at the person or persons that we blame for our former imprisonment. Grunts, groans, and guilt are common feelings here, but they don't have to last very long if we know to watch for them. I'm not saying to stuff them down, for that would put the cork back on the bottle, blocking our systems. If a push-pull comes up, we can work through it—or scream into a pillow instead.

During the unraveling of our potential, we may have a fresh lightness, a peace in our hearts from having reconnected with a brand new part of ourselves. But in the next moment, we may feel overwhelmed. We're newborn babes, buck naked in the wind, at least for an instant, hour, day or two, until our new footing takes hold.

Marla, a business executive, for years had put her signal aside as she did everything conceivable to keep the six-company partnership she was running alive. She'd been swimming upstream against the current in her efforts to unite the former competitors—running interference, mediating arguments, soothing tempers, and coordinating collaborations. When she reached the last of many dead ends, she came to her senses, threw out the white flag and recommended that the partnership be disbanded—her job along with it. Then she took some time to explore her interests and discovered a hidden talent for photography, an activity she loved. But how many times she came close to tossing away this passion, feeling vulnerable, exposed, and inexperienced, regardless of the number of ooh's and ah's she'd received from fans.

Consider the executives who face odd emotional hiccups when financial dreams come true, stock options mature, windfalls arrive, or personal goals are exceeded. After the sale of a company, for example, can come a surprising aftereffect, a sudden lack of identity. Who were they now that the company they'd run for so long was now running without them? Had they really made a difference all those years? Had their presence been as important as they'd once believed?

My first "buck naked" moment came over dinner in New York when a deeper connection suddenly surfaced with a woman I'd known for years. Between bites of linguini, my friend Jeanette and I found ourselves talking about business, philosophy, and, quite unexpectedly, our hearts. Without warning, we found ourselves asking, "Where had that other Sally and Jeanette pair gone, those twenty-somethings who delighted in putting on masks (quite literally) for the costume parties they so often threw?" Something disappeared that night as new facets of our signals took their chance to shine through. We were uncharacteristically shy as we said good-bye, the vulnerability at having revealed more than we'd intended having displaced the time-worn easiness of our relationship—luckily, not for long, though!

Surrounding us is a world of potential, of possibility, of light. A world in which each of us can take flight. A world in which expressing ourselves isn't our right, it's our responsibility.

When the push-pull sensation arrives for the first time, it can be quite disconcerting. But as the sensation becomes more familiar, you'll find a kind of comfort with it, knowing that it's a sure sign of forward movement. Fortunately, a good night's sleep usually resets you. Overachievers often learn to clear a hiccup away on the spot with a few deep breaths, a good belly laugh, or a nice warm cup of tea.

Then after any push-pull hiccup is out, the more fun job of retraining your muscles, restabilizing your stances, and reconnecting with the world in a new way begins. With room to breathe, space to play, and light to shine on us, it's time to stand up straight and tall, proud and free. And like a playful otter, colorful peacock, or with the gentle gawkiness of a newborn fawn, rediscover all that we really are.

casting out fear

Do you know the quote from Marianne Williamson's classic, *A Return To Love?* "*Our deepest fear is not that we are inadequate. Our deepest fear is that we are powerful beyond measure. It is our light, not our darkness, that most frightens us. We ask ourselves, 'Who am I to be brilliant, gorgeous, talented, fabulous?' Actually who are you not to be? Your playing small doesn't serve the world. There's nothing enlightened about shrinking so that other people won't feel insecure around you. . . As we let our own light shine, we unconsciously give other people permission to do the same. As we're liberated from our own fear, our presence automatically liberates others."*

There is no question that Marianne is speaking the truth. Shining is our natural right, a more natural state simply couldn't be. But how many times have we tried to express ourselves, to say something different, only to be told (more or less bluntly) that it's much better to fit in?

Take this moment to feel with me, to feel the power of a perfectly imperfect human being. Connect with the you who's reading this passage and feel the present size of your energetic skin. Are you shrunken like a raisin, beaten down from one too many of life's persistent knocks? This is your chance to change that if you'd like. Using your next breath as fuel, expand yourself out one full notch. It's not a puffing up that we're doing, it's a realignment of energies. Breathe in from the air itself a brand new possibility. . . that maybe, just maybe, humans are more than we were ever told we could be.

Surrounding us is a world of potential, of possibility, of light. A world in which each of us can take flight. A world in which expressing ourselves isn't our right, it's our responsibility.

Perhaps it's my analytical engineering brain, or perhaps my recklessly positive nature, but I've always searched for the light in a dark tunnel, the answer to even the most complicated puzzle, the hand that beats the odds and keeps the factory running. *I want to know under what conditions, and with what combination of parameters, is a spit-polished-no-holds-barred-shine made easy?*

Pretend that the difficulty of shining is just an illusion, a story we've been told, a drama that Hollywood has perfected in its effort to entertain. Imagine we've been tricked to believe that there needs to be a bad guy to make a good one stand out, a night to contrast the day. Let's say, for argument's sake, that the reported sixty percent of today's managers who think they've faked their way to the top are simply wrong. Inner confidence is common. Hearts are opened wide as well as minds. The unique gifts of each person are completely understood, and perfect roles for them found. One insult can't erase a dozen compliments anymore. Compliments and good feelings are here to stay. And to glow is easy, as natural a state as can ever be.

Before you laugh me out of the room, consider that virtually all of us have had the experience of shining, no matter how miserable, unfortunate, or loveless our lives might have generally been. It might have been something as simple as when you were sitting at the table with a friend, sketching designs on some loose-leaf paper, then realized that you were really pretty darned good. Smiles were exchanged. Perhaps a compliment or two. Time passed with no effort at all. Or the teacher who spurred you on. The coach or boss who saw your talent. The parent who smiled every time you walked in the room.

Maybe the childhood friend whom you loved with all your heart, who understood your thoughts before you even formulated them in your mind, brought out your most brilliant shine. We are happy at the thought of friends like these. Smiles overtake our faces, our features soften and glow. And if we stop for a minute to bring friends like this to mind right now, we would still find spots in our hearts dedicated specifically to them.

We are looking for the people who both get "it," in a general sense, and get "us" in particular.

completing the pass

The bulk of this chapter—in time spent, not heaviness— examines our relationships, the people we surround ourselves with. We are looking for the people who both get "it," in a

exposing her signal

a mom who matters

Before Michelle, a stay-at-home mother of four, was diagnosed with Hodgkin's disease, she felt a pressure building inside of her body, an inner sense of urgency that she didn't know what to do with. She clearly remembers feeling that unless she released the pressure somehow, she would get sick. Some weeks later, her doctors detected cancer in her lymphatic system.

She struggled to cure herself so she could get back to her family duties, and resume her normal routine. Then one day, an epiphany arrived. She realized that her job was, indeed, to cure herself, but that this cure would by its very nature undoubtedly *change* her routine. Her life as she knew it was over.

"I had the sudden realization that *I matter,*" she said. "That I *have* to take care of me—yes, for my family, but not only for my family. I have to take care of me or literally the pressure will continue to build inside of me and I'll be gone. The cancer will kill me unless I realize how much I matter." It's not an exaggeration to say that she'd never thought this way before, not even remotely. She'd been the perfect partner, the quintessential "martyr mom."

During Michelle's bout with cancer, relationships fascinated her. She was curious to see people's perceptions of her, and even more curious to see her perceptions of them. Before, someone else's opinion would have affected her deeply. She would have tried to adjust her signal, if you will, to match theirs. But her illness wouldn't allow her to do this anymore; she didn't have the strength, or, interestingly, the desire. She found herself watching the people who came to visit as if she were meeting them for the first time.

When people would cry at seeing her so fragile and weak, she didn't cry with them as she once might have. When they were uncomfortable, afraid to "catch" her cancer, she didn't move quickly to comfort them as was her habit. She let them move through the sensation on their own instead. It's not that she'd lost her compassion, quite the contrary. She'd simply become bigger than the white caps on other people's emotional waves. She'd become the lighthouse in her very own storm, a shining example of the peace she'd found in her most unusual situation.

Michelle had found a strength that she never knew she had. And each of the people who came to visit, even those who ran away, helped train her to sense her signal more fully than she'd ever had before.

"It's as if I started looking at myself from the outside," Michelle said, "seeing myself as someone else might see me. And recognizing how important it is that I'm here. Perhaps I'm loving myself in a new way; I don't know. I feel simple, true . . . and *raw*. Yes, raw is a very good word to use."

Truth—the pure, simple, and sometimes painful truth—was as obvious as a neon light to her. It led her through her illness, and then became the fuel on which she lived. Any insincerities, hollow words, or false compliments fell right by the wayside, along with conclusions that were jumped to, fears that posed as facts, and promises that she knew would not be kept. She had no time for or interest in them. She spent her time, instead, distinguishing which were the truest connections among her family and friends, and learning more about who she was with each and every connection she made.

general sense, and get "us" in particular. Rather than keeping on the "straight and narrow," we want to identify those precious few who set us loose on the "powerfully-aligned, opened, and expanded." People you can count on, like my Jessica.

Perhaps it's my cultural roots speaking, since Italians intuitively understand the value of being in good company. To my cousins, the idea of me having lived alone for so long is, quite frankly, absurd. They simply wouldn't do it, couldn't conceive of it. It's considered unnatural. A good half of single Italians stay home until they marry—even if that's at thirty-five or forty years old.

Americans are more independent as a culture. We like to do things ourselves, to conquer that goal, to go after that dream. But maybe it's time to soften ourselves up a bit, and add to our life survival list—food, water, shelter, and *avere compagnia,* having some nice company around.

Lest you be concerned that by counting on another person you'll completely lose your independence, pick up some pop-psych affliction, or be imposing on someone's generosity, let me reassure you that giving this kind of support is anything but burdensome. The force of two people making a genuine connection completes a magical circuit that can change the world. It's an equal exchange, a two-way street. Both sides benefit. So instead of this being a help-yourself-to-yourself book, let's call it a help-yourself-to-yourself-and-each-other book. Yes, that sounds just about right.

Humans are social creatures, after all. We need each other. So when we're feeling stuck, raw, naked, or unsure of what's beyond the next bend in our road, as the genuinely imperfect humans that we are, let's take the time to connect with someone who both gets "it" and gets the real "us." And let's not stop until we find someone who has more confidence in us than we have in ourselves.

Yes, you heard me right. These people exist. They come in all kinds of packages—called friends, grandparents, neighbors, children, teachers, parents, therapists, leaders, ministers . . . or even the occasional stranger on the street. They may be men or women, teenagers, or retirees. They may be bosses, colleagues, or several rungs down on the corporate ladder. They may use many words or they may use few. They may see you often, maybe not. The common element is that you feel a connection with them, often an instant one. And that both of you are willing to make this connection real, to say what needs to be said.

It was Jessica who sat by me during my illness, watching the light go in and out of my eyes. She didn't run away from the fear that she sometimes felt, nor did she amplify the fear that was boiling up inside of me. She just stayed with me, participating in the mystery, making me feel less like a freak and more like a whole human being.

Looking back to each critical moment of my life, there was always a person who was by my side. My aunt who was the nurse in the room at my birth, and who has managed to always understand me, no matter how often I've changed. My gymnastics coach who saw my deeper side, and introduced me to philosophy. Jessica's father who encouraged me to go into the non-technical side of technology. "We need you there," he said, with a sparkle in his eye.

Each of these people saw something in me that I hadn't yet seen in myself. Each of them, in their own way, helped bring out my shine.

Shining can be as simple as smiling your most natural smile or it may take a more tangible form like winning a Nobel prize or getting a big promotion. Have you seen the e-mail that asked you to name the last five winners of a number of prizes like these? It's pretty hard to do. But when asked to identify the people who've most influenced you—the teachers who encouraged you, your best friends over the years, the person who said the right thing at just the right time, the heroes who inspired you—it's easy. They are the people who made the difference to you *personally.*

People who both get "it" and get "you," who shine as beacons of unfiltered light, are the fairies of the fairy tales, the dwarves and elves who show up with the magic beans and the sparkling incantation, as my friend Agnes (a pixie in her own right) likes to say. "I couldn't have done it without you," we hear ourselves respond. And, once again, we would be absolutely right.

"You have to *complete the pass,*" one such fairy tale-like acquaintance said to me one day while sitting in my living room. "There's something in making a connection that's important beyond the mere physical nature of the act." The power of his words noticeably stirred him. How something so simple could hold such a force.

Having our words heard, our affection returned, and our opinions appreciated (even if they're not agreed with or even understood!) is potent. There's a magic in the air, a ball of energy, a sweet aroma. A contact is made, a present received, a communication completed. There's mutual respect and an agreement for both people to be exactly who they are—freely. We learn a bit more about ourselves with every completed pass. It's invigorating. It brings life more alive.

Through the completeness of our connections, we discover for either the first time, or simply remember again, all that we really are.

Ask any actor on the stage, poll any speaker. The audience makes a difference, it counts. It's no secret that it's more enjoyable to cook for two. Or that we're more apt to buy products from someone we like. Advertisers have known this for years. Every writer knows that the best articles are written with the end publication already in mind. Audiences can want you to fail and you just may, or they can ride that thrill along with you in their encouragement for you to succeed. Just like a teacher can make things more difficult or easy to learn.

By contrast, a little bit of you can die when you throw a pass and it hits the ground, ignored, bouncing in some crazy direction for you to chase after. Such effort. Such annoyance. So much work for so little in return.

I can hear some of you asking, "But do we always need other people around to be able to shine our brightest? Do incomplete passes have to hurt?" In one word, *no.* In Walk (Step 4), in fact, we'll become *palle pazze* (crazy bouncy balls) and learn to effortlessly recover after a fall. Then in Fly (Step 6), we'll learn to harness the energy of the fall itself to spring back with even more vitality than before. With practice, we can glow locked in a closet alone. And if a pass isn't caught? Who cares. Just ignore that glazed look in the other person's eye, and move on.

But for those of us not used to shining, who aren't really sure that what we have to say has value, who don't have our energetic muscles trained, the best way to polish our shine is to connect with another genuinely imperfect human being. There is something about that initial eye-to-eye connection that satisfies an inner hunger and creates the drive to shine each and every day. Through the completeness of our connections, we discover for either the first time, or simply remember again, all that we really are.

Then it's absolutely *simple* to shine.

let the games begin: Imagine a playground filled with people of every shape, size, and temperament. Twinkling eyes, dancing feet, genuine smiles . . . and limitless time. Go find your friends. Run all you want in this playground. Fly. Soar.

1. sunshine *(1 minute):* Men and women both, imagine yourself, right now, on the beach in Sicily, sporting a string bikini, soaking up the sunshine. If it makes you more comfortable, let your mind's eye take five, fifteen, or fifty pounds off your body before you slip that bikini on. Ladies, I'm not talking about a prudent two-piece with just an inch of flesh showing, like the ones my friends usually bring when they visit (and my cousin Patrizia promptly laughs at). I mean one of those itsy bitsy ones, the kind I never would have dared wear past the age of twenty-five, the real thing. Your size, age, or weight don't matter here. This is the Mediterranean!

2. cover up *(2 minutes):* Think back to the kinds of things you did as a kid just to fit in. I used to get called "scrawny legs" in elementary school and began to wear pants instead of the dresses I'd loved. In a hurry to get breasts, I began eating past my point of comfort, following the lead of the heavy-set girl who sat behind me in band who was already popping out. Then after I saw a girl smiling brightly on the school bus one day, I decided to perpetually plaster on a smile of my own, hoping I could at least *look* as happy as she clearly felt.

Please don't let me be the only silly one here. I love company, as you know. Can you remember one specific thing you did as a kid to cover up? Did you move beyond it . . . or is part of it still with you today?

3. kid stuff *(2 minutes):* What encouragement, if any, did you receive as a child? And from whom? As a kid I once wrote a page of poetry—you know, about important things like the Easter bunny and my cat. I remember being so proud of myself. But all I got from my mom was a quick "how nice" before she raced off to tend to one of my siblings. My poetry career began and ended that day . . . then rejuvenated itself a full twenty years later when I found that very same page, saved by one very proud mom.

At the beginning of a new road, encouragement can hold a magic power. Once my dad told me that his best present ever was a birthday card that I'd sent, one with words that I'd tearfully written inside. Little did he know that I'd regretted sending it just after having dropped it into the mail. His surprising encouragement enticed me to write even more.

If you can't remember any examples from childhood, perhaps you can remember a friend or boss who said just the right thing at just the right time, spurring you to start or continue on a new path. As the final part of this exercise, ask yourself if there is a person in your life who's trying something new whom you can encourage right now. A few minutes are all you need to complete the pass.

4. describe yourself *(5 minutes):* Fill an entire page with adjectives that describe you. You know, words like pretty, funny, intelligent, agile, scatterbrained, peppy, bossy, dopey, goofy. Don't stop until the page is full. Overachievers, whip out a fresh piece of paper and fill that, too.

Now, write down things you're really good at. Yes, loading the dishwasher counts. Or finding the best program on TV, no matter what time of day it is. But I know you can do better than that. Go for it. Fill the page—or more.

words that describe me	things i'm good at

simply singing her song

rosie's dream

When Rosie was in her role as Internet executive, she was the conductor of an orchestra, leading an entire section of strings. But when she visited me in Sicily the year I was writing this book, she had a much easier, but no less critical (at least to me!) role to play.

I'd been stuck in a writer's block, too many thoughts trying to find a place in too few pages. I was searching for the center of the center, the bellybutton of my work, the diamond's raw natural brilliance. That was exactly the moment that Rosie arrived. Happy for the distraction, I put my writings down and played.

On her very last day there, Rosie awoke with memories of a dream she'd had. She'd been preparing for a role in a play. It was a teeny tiny part. "But the fuss they made in rehearsal," she exclaimed, "when I sang my one silly line!" She was sure that the conductor had overdone his praise, that she'd barely be noticed during the actual performance. But after her line was successfully delivered to her dream-time audience, they rose to their feet and *roared!*

"Could this be so?" Rosie thought. "Could it really be this easy?"

Yes, it could. And after Rosie left for the air-port, I began writing the very next day.

5. being described (*5 minutes*)*:* It's often easier for someone to see us than for us to see ourselves. Ask at least three people to give you, off the top of their heads, three adjectives that describe you . . . and three things you are really good at. Family members, friends, people at work, your dentist . . . pick any three, then ask. Make it simple. Make it fun. And be sure to pick people who are both sensitive in general and care about you in particular. Did they notice any things about you that you missed?

6. 10,000-watt shine *(3 minutes):* Describe one moment in your life when you felt happy, full, when you had a rich, sparkling glow.

7. don't worry, be happy *(1 minute):* One summer in Sicily, a local guy asked me out. My cousins, in their effort to protect me, drilled me about his intentions, education, and background, then recited a long list of worries, everything that could possibly go wrong. The lightness I'd felt at the original invitation all but left my body. "Relax," I said. "It's just a first date. I don't even know if there'll be a second!"

Can you think of an instance when people dumped a bunch of fears on you when all you wanted was for them to be happy for you? Or when someone's jealousy caused you to shrink and keep your good news to yourself?

8. real support, part one *(10 minutes):* It's time to get to the heart of the matter—your relationships. Notice the drawing of concentric circles on this page (it looks like the ripples in a pond after a pebble was thrown in). Put the names of the people closest to you, whom you see every day, in the inner-most circle. Then in the next circle out, write the names of people you're the next closest to, like those you work with or see only on the holidays. Go out as many circles as you'd like, even enough to include your doctor, hairdresser, or insurance agent. Then when you're done, circle the names of the people who give you energy just thinking about them.

9. real support, part two *(5 minutes):* Now let's go a little deeper. Take that same chart that you just made and put a star next to the names of the people *who support you for simply being you.* No performing. No dramas. Just whole-hearted support. When you think about these people, it often feels like a combination of your energy lifting and your heart singing—no "work" is required.

Overachievers, compare the names from the last exercise to this one. Are there any people who give you energy when you think about them, but somehow don't support you for being you? Is this possible? Perhaps they are fun to be around but want you to be somehow different than who you really are . . . or want only one or two of your facets to show, not the whole you. We're searching for the people who require no special energy output at all. The ones that when we get together, we seem to *generate* energy.

Let me be clear that the goal of these exercises is to open your perspective, not to shed all of the people who drain your energy. In fact, over the years, I've noticed how some energy drainers turn into energy givers, and vice versa. The energy dynamic is indeed dynamic—seeding itself, sprouting, blossoming, shedding its leaves. The point is to notice who's who at this moment, make choices accordingly, and keep your mind open for the possibility of future change.

10. real support, part three (*3 minutes*): Many people view good support as someone who'll listen to all of your woes, pull you out of a hole, and protect you from anything, including yourself. They'll laugh with you, cry with you, gossip with you . . . in short, never leave your side.

Now let's open this view a magical half degree, and define good support as someone who can see your signal in the noise *and not let you forget it.* No matter how chaotic your life may be in a given moment, they are your lighthouse in the storm. They see right where you are, no matter how low you've gone, and still hold you as strong. Their perspective is broad, unwavering, and often has a good sense of humor attached. They tell you the truth even when it's painful. They hold out their hands from the top of the hole you're in, encouraging you to climb out by yourself. And when you finally get there, they are the first to applaud.

My friend Soleira is like this. She sees only my signal, she won't even respond to any noise. If I send her an e-mail filled with a mixture of doubts and dreams, she'll graciously respond only to the dreams, letting my insecurities go totally ignored, completely unfed.

Do you have a friend like this? Who doesn't get sucked down your energy drain, fooled by the masks you wear, the distances you keep, the excuses you use, or your self-protective routines? If so, with your next in-breath, let your friend's clarity resonate with your own, filling your body from your head to your toes. If you can't identify a friend with these qualities, open to the possibility that one day soon you will.

11. body scan *(1 minute):* From where you are seated or lying down right now, feel how your body is touching the surface it is sitting or resting on. Now, imagine that your full weight is being supported by the hands of the wisest, most generous, and respectful person you know—or someone you wish you knew. Think big, feel his or her connection with you . . . then relax into the sensation. Let the powerful hands hold you, supporting you, and taking all of your tensions away.

12. take the show on the road *(10 seconds):* We often lose our humanity as we turn into machines behind the wheel of our cars, trucks, and SUVs. Let's flip this around. The next time you are merging into traffic, try looking the other driver— the one who's not making it at all easy for you to squeeze in— squarely, directly, kindly, and gently in the eyes. If each of us spent just ten seconds connecting with someone in this way, I bet we'd see road rage diminish, if not disappear altogether.

13. completing the pass *(5 minutes):* Relationships are undoubtedly our richest learning ground. Using the following scenarios as a guide, take a look at the people that you've interacted with over the years and see if you can learn something more about who you really are. Jot down your answers in the margin of this page.

- **FULL FORCE.** Who can you be your full 10,000 watts around, not having to dim your bulb even slightly, not even one little bit?
- **PULL YOU OUT.** Who can really get you talking, pull you right out?
- **FAMILY TIES.** Who inspired you to keep pursuing your interests when they peeked out for the first time?
- **EASY DOES IT.** Who can slow you down, relax you, make even the most hectic day somehow okay?
- **OUT OF THE BOX.** Who has been successful getting you to do something completely uncharacteristic for you?
- **TEACHERS, COACHES, BOSSES.** Which of them brought a new skill out in you, saw your potential before you did . . . or challenged you to stretch, break new ground, reach a new level in a skill you already had?
- **ACTORS, AUTHORS, POLITICIANS, ACTIVISTS.** You don't have to personally know people to connect with them. Which people or books have opened, inspired, or encouraged you?
- **MUSIC, SPORTS, FASHION, BOOKS, ADVENTURES, ART.** Are there any particular people you enjoy doing your hobbies with?
- **TOUGH TIMES AND CRITICISM.** Which people got you through your top three toughest times? Who had the courage to tell you the hard truth to help turn a situation around?

- **FUN AND VACATIONS.** In each decade of your life, which people did you have the most fun with?
- **GROUP DYNAMICS.** Classes offer a connection for people with the same curiosity. Support groups bring people together who are facing similar situations. Community and church groups offer a chance to connect. What group experiences have you had that have either made you feel connected in a fresh way or brought out a new interest in you?
- **DARE TO BE DIFFERENT.** Who is the person you've connected with that has the personality, culture, or background most different from your own?

14. bringing heart to the matter *(5 minutes):* Bring your awareness to your heart (putting your hands there will help) and as fast as you can, write down everything you can think of that would make that very heart sing. What you love to do, even if you haven't done it for a while (or ever). Go wild. Break the rules. Get out of the box. And make sure at least some of the items would take less than five minutes to do. Then the next time it's convenient, do the *easiest possible one.*

15. buck naked in the wind *(1 minute):* After a sudden change, a success, a new facet of yourself appearing, your 10,000 watt shine lighting up the world around you, you can sometimes get the push-pull sensation of feeling vulnerable, raw, buck naked in the wind. These are the "hiccup" moments where you doubt your identity because this very identity is in the process of changing to something brand new. You may get sad, confused, act out, want to hide or go back to your old life, doubting what the new life in front of you is really offering.

Think for a moment if you've ever experienced a sensation like this before, big or little, momentary or lingering . . . or if you're experiencing one now. And know that it's perfectly natural if you have. How long did it stay with you? A few minutes, days, weeks, or years?

16. the changing of the guard *(1 minute):* There are very few things in life more painful than losing a treasured relationship. But virtually every big change requires a good hard look at the people to whom you are closest. Is there someone in your innermost circle who is draining your energy or in some way holding you back?

17. outside in *(as long as you'd like):* Until this point, we've been using our feeling nature from the *inside out* to polish our shines. Now let's work from the *outside in.* Do something to enhance your physical appearance, to suit the new, fresh, real, and glorious you. This could be as simple as taking a nice, refreshing shower with your favorite soap, polishing your shoes, or getting a pedicure. Or as extravagant as going to a spa for a complete makeover. Overachievers, go buy yourself a new outfit, too.

wrap-up

We each have a gift to share, a 10,000 watt light bulb that's just waiting to turn on. With practice, this light can shine every single day. But at first, it takes the magic of a connection, the completion of an electrical circuit if you will, to start the flow of that inner glow. In this chapter we looked from many different angles at the ways we interact with others, and just what types of interactions pull out the best in us—enhancing our shine and bringing our fullest selves out to share with the world.

step 4, walk

GOAL: STAY YOURSELF MORE EACH DAY. *With our "noise" at record-low levels, our "signals" standing tall and proud, it's time to walk down our new paths. In this step we walk the line between being true to ourselves and fitting in. We discover a variety of ways to pick ourselves up after a fall. And we learn when to hold out hope for something or belief in someone . . . and when it's best for everyone to just walk away.*

The Sicilians have these great toy balls for sale in big, colorful, fishbowl-like, put-a-coin-in-and-voilà! machines. A crazy ball pops out, *una palla pazza*. Kids love them, and so do I. What's most interesting about these balls is that with practically no force at all on your part, they bounce right back up to the place from which you drop them. The engineer in me marvels at their near-perfect elasticity. The kid in me just loves to watch them go. In this step we're going to become like *palle pazze*. When life puts a rock in our path and we trip over it, we're going to bounce right back up. When we feel a heaviness in our heart or on our shoulders, we're going to slough it right off. The goal is to stay our light, bright, shining selves more hours of every day.

Sure, we'll have down times, too. As genuinely imperfect human beings, we often find ourselves going in and out of our real selves many times each day. One minute we're "off" and the next we're "on." We get down on ourselves, then lighten up. We lose perspective momentarily, then find it again. We have a wave of tiredness come over us, then feel a resurgence of new energy. We argue, sulk, cry, or complain—naturally. But by the end of this step, we'll recover sooner from the things life throws our way, keeping more clear and balanced on a more consistent basis. The goal is to have our signals as clear as they felt at the end of Clean (Step 2), and as shiny as at the end of Polish (Step 3), and to keep any new dirt, dust, heaviness, or grime from getting on them. Or, when it does, from staying there too long. Flexibility, agility, and a spring in our step is what we're going for.

There is no schedule for soul movement. There is no grand plan. There is only the movement created by the invitation of a clear mind and sincerely-opened heart, combined with the choices we make.

The most insidious enemies we face during a typical day come from our brains in the form of lingering doubts, repetitious mind games, and mundane worries that tie us up in knots. Since decisive and playful forward movement is what this step is all about, out of our brains we will go and dive straight into our hearts.

Our hearts know who we are, no matter what's happening in our outer world. Our hearts have a built-in confidence that we are indeed splendid in measure, capability, and size. One of the most important outcomes of this chapter is to get our heads to understand this, too, and to accept that the ebb and flow of the natural human day brings us forward, ever so gently, and at times with a major growth spurt.

Humans, by nature, are not just simple creatures, dutifully marching along, singing the same song day in and day out. We are organic beings that can change speeds at will, move, and evolve. We're entire instruments, whole melodies, complete symphonies. At times we skip, at other times stand tall. At times we voice deep rhythmic tones, like the beat of a bass drum, and at other times piercing notes, like the clear voice of a single piccolo. Each velocity, each note, is a different facet of our lives. And each facet has a time and place to come out, a season under the sun.

It takes but one quick look at nature to see evidence of the natural cycle of life. Winter's internal focus is needed to store enough energy for spring. Days follow nights, sunrises follow sunsets. Planted seeds take a full season to grow. And our planet takes one year to complete its solar cycle.

If our planet tried to rush, it would look a little silly, wouldn't it? Yet humans try to rush all the time, scurrying in the city streets and passing each other like maniacs on the freeway. We want to know the answers before the questions have even been properly formulated. We want to know if a relationship will work out even before we've gone on a first date. Every time we rush, we throw ourselves off balance and lose a little more contact with what's happening around us. Pleading, forcing, pushing, trying, striving, clinging, worrying . . . these are all ways to fixate a mind, close a heart, trap a soul, and lose more precious moments of ourselves in a day.

As we refocus our minds enough to listen to our hearts, our souls break free to bring out new facets and move us as they move themselves. There is no schedule for soul movement. There is no grand plan. There is only the movement created by the invitation of a clear mind and sincerely-opened heart, combined with the choices we make.

When we are most ourselves, most balanced and relaxed, it's less easy for us to get angry, and almost impossible for someone to suck us into an argument. We listen, we reflect, we argue, we banter, we agree to disagree. We breathe fully, we laugh more. Our bodies talk to us freely. We feel these bodies, understand their language, and follow what they have to say—even if no one else sees it the very same way. We go on with our day, appreciating its company, and knowing that another day is waiting its turn to arrive.

harmonizing our facets

Perhaps you've heard the saying, *"Dance like no one is watching, sing like no one is listening, and love like you've never been hurt."* When I showed this to a man I was dating, these nineteen words brought the senior executive to his knees, the look of panic on his face greater than any fear he'd had of death by fire or a business deal gone wrong. Compare that to when I translated the saying for my ten-year-old *cuginetta* (cousin) Amelia. She just looked at me curiously, not sure what I'd been trying to say. Sure, she'd be shy at times to read her English lessons to me, but to put limits on dancing or love? This concept was completely foreign to her, as it would be to any well-loved child around the world. She just smiled politely, then tucked the gift away in a drawer.

In this step we'll find our most natural strides, then strike up the marching band. We'll learn to stay ourselves for more hours of every day—despite anyone watching, any negativity or disappointment to wade through, any problems to resolve, or any daily duties or routines.

When my *cuginetta* Amelia dances she's a sparkling wind chime, arms and feet flailing about. When she slows her pace down to paint, she transforms into the wise, long notes of the orchestra's bass, pulling together the colors, images, and sounds of the entire orchestra, content to be all by herself. Her child's face turns contemplative, her touch sure. When Amelia whips herself into a fury, gaze sharp and defiant, arms crossed, she becomes a blast of a well-tuned French horn. She is all of these things, and a few others at times, her own instrument created, her unique harmony defined.

Part of you may be a plodding tuba, while another part is a frolicking flute. If you are like Amelia, you'd be perfectly content with that, annoyed or bored only if the part of you that wanted to make a big trumpet blare was being kept from singing that tune. You'd know instinctively that the world needs all instruments for its band. And you'd know exactly which ones you like to be, as well as the ones you like to hang around.

I once heard someone try to take the spring out of Amelia's step by telling her that a painting she'd been planning would be very hard to do. Amelia believed her (at least momentarily), and then repeated the warning to me. "Just tell me one time when painting *anything* was hard for you!" I replied. Her smile brightened, the invisible weight lifted, and she skipped off to play.

Walking, running, skipping, jumping, frolicking, leapfrogging, crawling, strutting, plodding, slinking, standing, leaping, hopping, tiptoeing, kneeling, strolling, prowling, sliding, dancing, spinning, lying down, sitting . . . Look at how many choices we have in our day.

accepting disharmony

Just as there is a certain pace that legs the size of yours naturally move, there are certain instruments that you best harmonize with and others that you don't. Or in human terms, some people (or aspects of them) that at best get on your nerves and at worst throw you completely off balance. In Italy there's an expression: *"Smussare gli angoli,"* smooth out the corners.

It suggests that we can't change anyone's basic character: people are who they are, and that's that. So if there are aspects of people that grate on us, the best we can hope for is that one day (not even soon) they'll round off their sharp edges a bit.

Acceptance is the undercurrent of the Italian culture, the fullness of being human the fabric of Italy's being. As a culture, Italy celebrates every lump, curve, and scent, each bite of food on its plate, and each sip of wine on its lips. Bikinis are for anyone who'd like to wear them. Odd birds decorate the genealogical tree. Families usually live near each other and eat together often. Family businesses are common things. Sure, Italians complain, talk behind each other's backs, and can be judgmental. But they also count on each other and have perfected the art of accepting the complete characters, the perfect imperfections, of the people they love.

Take my cousin Patrizia's husband, for example. His oddity is that he's been known to leave his own dinner parties half way through, with guests seated at the table in the middle of eating the food. "To do what?" you ask? To go to sleep or watch TV. Conversation often bores him, it's the cooking that he likes to do. The first time this happened Patrizia was a young bride, and the dinner table had been filled with *his* friends, not hers. She was mortified. "That's just Raffaele," his friends laughed. "He always does that." No problem.

Are Italians crazy, over-indulgent, or just plain wrong to be so accepting of themselves and others? Or have they found a secret short-cut, a sincere way to let imperfections harmlessly slide off and not get in anyone's way?

With over fifty governments since World War II and the 2000-year-old Roman Empire to refer back to, perhaps the Italians have just seen more of life than we have, are more familiar with its twists, turns, ups, and downs. Maybe the

Americans are just teenagers to the Italian eyes, impetuous youth who think they can conquer the world. The Italians may be wiser from having been both conqueror and conquered so many times. Perhaps they understand that the real war to win is the battle to find peace in our own hearts and comfort inside our very own skin.

the whole picture

acceptance, italian-style

When my cousin Pina's parents refused to send her to the athletic-oriented high school to pursue the sports she loved, she felt cut off at the knees. "I'll take the bus a half hour each way, *Papà. Non vi preoccupate!*" she pleaded, but to no avail. They wanted her to focus on studies instead.

Pina didn't like to study, she loved working with her natural physical strength. "My critical moment came when I got older, finally told my family no and started doing things my own way," she said, remembering with pride the moment she declared herself free. "But soon after that, I surprised myself," she added with a twinkle in her eye. "I suddenly found it perfectly fine to say yes. Why, you ask? Let me see . . . It's because at that point I knew who I was, separate from my family. I'd found *me.*"

To Pina, the moment that most builds people's character, that strengthens their signal, is when they first separate from the people they love—whether it's by conscious choice or not (through a death, for example). When we as people are pulled apart, we see ourselves as distinct from each other, then have the chance to see what kind of choices we make. Through our series of choices, step by step, we find ourselves.

If you ask her what her future holds, she'll look at you with a smile. "I love to cook, it relaxes me. I love all of the things I have here—my husband, my children, my plants, the house herself. I love things to be simple, and the simplest of things . . . The rest? It holds no interest for me."

As that thought is whirling around your brain, let's change continents and reach back further in time to look at a 3,000-year-old Far Eastern Taoist text, poem No. 57 of the *Hua Hu Ching*. It shows another angle on the subject of accepting life's peculiarities, in energetic terms. Feel your energy cup as you read these next lines.

The universe is a vast net of energy rays . . .

By integrating the positive, harmonious energy rays with the positive elements of your own being, and eliminating the subtle negative influences, you can enhance all aspects of your life.

In order to eliminate the negative influences, simply ignore them . . .

Its approach is beautiful, honest, and sincere. Become aware of the energy states around you. Be conscious of them in every moment of your day. Surround yourself with positive influences, bask in them, draw them to you. And simply ignore any negative ones. Don't water them or feed them, don't spend time fixing or fighting them, don't give them even one bit of encouragement or power.

"You just *ignore* them, Jessica," I practically screamed into the phone one day, minutes after having read the poem for the first time. "It's so simple. He's a genius." In fact, Jessica would learn this same lesson herself when raising her first child. When Juliet fussed over something, Jessica would gently draw Juliet's attention to something that the little one enjoyed. No commotion made. Current problem solved.

Some may argue that an Italian or Taoist-style acceptance may not easily translate to American soil. With our big-better-best-never-let-it-rest culture, it may be hard to accept the full-bodied wholeness of a person we love, and just ignore the rest.

Americans thrive on continuously improving our products, homes, businesses, careers, and personalities. The idea of letting loved ones simply be who they are (rough edges and all), that we can be genuinely imperfect humans who get along *most* of the time, takes a little wind out of our sails, doesn't it? Feel that with me and see.

But does it have to? Is there space in the American culture for solid whole-hearted acceptance? Let's try an experiment, a short meditation, and see if we can find some room for this view. As you read these words, imagine that you are in a relationship (friendship, romance, job, family, pet) that's great most of the time. No, he or she doesn't beat you or anything horrible like that. It's just that every once in a while you feel a bit out-of-synch, unappreciated, or misunderstood. You know what I'm talking about. Take whatever your particular annoyance is with this other person, persons, or pet and let it fill a television screen in your mind. Take as long as you want to get the picture very, very clear.

Now, keeping your eye on the screen, take five giant steps backwards. With each step visualize the picture on the screen becoming bigger and more balanced in its view. Put the less-than-ideal aspects of your relationship into perspective with all of the good things that it offers. Take all the time you need to watch your mental picture change.

If you find yourself resisting the bigger picture, bring your attention to your head, and consciously breathe three big breaths straight into it, asking it to calm down. If the picture needs even more perspective, bring your attention to your heart and consciously breathe three big breaths straight into it, asking it to open a little more widely. Then with three new breaths aimed right at that television screen in your mind's eye, keep adjusting until an honest picture is formed.

Now, ask yourself, on balance, is this relationship something you can accept *just as it is?* Only you can decide.

For acceptance to have power, it must be genuine, complete, and completely sincere. We can't settle for anything in a life that's alive, or put blind eyes to faults. Neither will do. What we need instead is a recognition of the "good" and "bad" things that we've got, and the fact that both will change over time. If our mates aren't perfect, we round out our lives with our buddies, colleagues, and friends. If we don't have enough money, we make do with just change. Then with a bigger perspective than we've ever had before, an appreciation of the many facets of the human gemstone can be born. We become bigger than any individual relationship or thing, we break through our chains, and we sprout wings.

The more we let roll off our shoulders—*honestly*—without sacrificing, shrinking, or stuffing even the smallest bit of ourselves, the more real, peaceful, creative, and productive we can be. We are already enough, and so are they. In fact, we are magnificent.

doors open, doors close

Now let's take a walk around the word "acceptance" to view it from the other side. Let's pretend that we are that great friend, parent, grandparent, coach, partner, teacher, boss, client, co-worker, or general fan that sees something great in a particular person, a potential they are blind to, a real prize. We want to bring it out and take it all the way to the goal line. But they don't see it as we do. They prefer to stay covered up. They aren't ready. They hold firm.

We have a danger of losing ourselves in our attempt to help others. Trying to open a locked door to which another person has the key is throwing our energy down the drain. It simply doesn't work.

You can't believe it. You go crazy. You try everything to

get them to see what is so obvious to you, to embrace their talents with a passion, if only they would try. But they turn a deaf ear, or worse yet, start a fight. They don't want to go there, they tell you, at least not yet. They have no interest in stepping through the door that you've opened so wide. They walk away, in fact—then slam the door shut. And miracle worker that you are, you sit there, stupefied, the sweet music you were offering falling into an unused pile of notes at your side.

We have a danger of losing ourselves in our attempt to help others. Trying to open a locked door to which another person has the key is throwing our energy down the drain. It simply doesn't work. As much as you believe in the potential of the person, as much as you'd like that satisfying sensation of being part of a freshly completed pass, you have to step aside. If another person isn't both open and engaged, you're in a game without a partner, holding both tennis rackets in one set of hands. The other person needs to be *ready, willing, and able—all three*—to step beyond any self-doubt, self-pity, self-medication, self-imprisonment, self-hatred, or general self-destruction. It's their life, their choice, their timing. Period.

As hard as it might be, when someone else chooses to stay stuck, it's usually best to walk away. Pounding the door down will only help in the most extreme of circumstances, to stop a suicide, for example. For the more common cases like a wasted life, passion, opportunity, or skill, until the other person is ready, willing, and able, no amount of pleading, pushing, shoving, or forcing will get them there. So drop the game ball, put the tennis racquets away. Give up the fight.

Then, as the Italians would say without skipping so much as one beat of life's choir, *"Si chiude una porta, si apre un portone,"* when one door closes on you, a bigger one opens. Every single time.

A "walk" is a deliberate action, a flexible movement, an unhurried stroll down a familiar street, an adventurous prowl through a less familiar part of town. We walk into trouble at times, just as we walk away from trouble at others. We go on walks by ourselves, which can be fun, or still more fun yet, we walk with someone else, arm-in-arm or hand-in-hand. At times we walk straight into brick walls. And we can find ourselves walking in circles a bit before we walk away once again, free and clear.

Being comfortable in the walk of life doesn't mean living without challenges, taking the easy path. It means knowing that no matter which path you're on, as long as you stay connected with your inner self, you're going to make it just fine. It's a confidence and an agility, a strength and a flexibility, a tension that both aggravates you and pulls the best out of you as it propels you forward. It's the place where criticism helps you rather than knocks you out. Where street vendors can cajole you, but not shake you. Where the sweet words of a gigolo can be enjoyed for just what they are. There are no statements to make except when you want to take a stand. No angst, no edge, no charge to your day. There is just you, your innate nature, sincere interests, odd oddities, and inner vitality humming away—and the people you love who walk at your side.

Being comfortable in the walk of life doesn't mean living without challenges, taking the easy path. It means knowing that no matter which path you're on, as long as you stay connected with your inner self, you're going to make it just fine.

let the games begin: To prepare for our walk, put your arms up, reaching your hands up high, feeling the stretch the whole way down your back to your toes. Do it again, adding a nice breath of your favorite size. Let the games begin!

1. limber up *(30 seconds):* Take off your shoes. Throw your pencil or pen on the floor and pick it up using only your toes.

2. set your own pace *(3 minutes):* Write down five musical instruments that best describe your various facets, the variety of ways that you present yourself to the world. Or if you're less of a musical type, choose five animals, colors, or flowers that best describe you. Or if you're the movement-oriented type, choose five different strides: walking, running, hiding, shuffling, or gliding, for example. There's no need to analyze anything, just have fun playing with how you'd imagine different aspects of yourself in a new way.

3. your first step *(2 minutes):* Bring to mind something you really, really want. Then ask yourself "What is the smallest possible step I can take in that direction?" It could be to unbury your art supplies from the back of the closet, desk, or drawer. To put film in your camera. To update your resume. To write a new sales brochure. To give her a hug. To give him a call. To put the first brick in a new sidewalk—physical or metaphoric. The first brushstroke on a canvas. A new file in the computer. Or simply locating a computer that you can use if you don't have one yourself. There are literally millions of choices.

Now walk, don't run, toward this thing that you really, really want. Take that critical first small step in your new direction. Think big, and start small.

teeny tiny next step

4. keep walking *(2 minutes):* Once that ice is broken, the first critical step taken, a new flow begins. Our job becomes to follow that flow, to put the pedal to the metal, and to navigate any blind curves. There's a cavernous moving walkway in Chicago's O'Hare airport that might be able to help. Its colorful neon lights cascade, turning on and off, playfully guiding you through the maze of United Airlines gates. A woman's voice whispers, *"Keep walking, keep walking . . . "* in time with soft music. Pretend you're on this walkway right now, and identify the next three teeny tiny steps toward your goal. Write them down. Overachievers, do one step each day for three days.

5. positive influences *(3 minutes):* Think of people (or just one person) who have had a positive influence on you. Write down what you appreciate about them—adjectives that describe them, fun times you had together, conversations you remember, a specific impact they had on you. The way they didn't let you run away that day when you were mad. The hard truth they told you, that all the others had shied away from. The belly laughs that you shared. An inside joke or two. Have fun.

6. negative influences *(2 minutes):* Now let's try the opposite. Identify people (or just one person) who are most definitely less than perfect. Then write down their very best qualities . . . and their very worst. Tell me honestly, do the pluses outweigh the minuses?

7. achilles heel *(3 minutes):* One day by complete surprise I found out just how much energy I'd been spending worrying. I was experimenting with a guided meditation into a past life and suddenly found myself as an Indian woman by a gently flowing stream. There were small pebbles under my deerskin-clad feet. One of my children was in sight, the other was around the bend. I was safe and so were they. There were no thoughts of the past, no concerns for the future. And for perhaps the first time in my life, I felt absolutely, positively worry-free. I wasn't worried about anyone else, *and no one else was worried about me.*

What exactly is it that worries you? Write it down, being as specific as possible. If it's "health," detail which aspects of your health are your greatest concern. If it's that "you won't find a partner," detail the reasons why you think that's so. Is it that you're afraid you're not attractive enough? Or that out of the billions of people in the world there isn't even *one* for you? After your list is complete, circle the worries that you still think are true.

Overachievers, write down *how* you worry—the route the thoughts take in your brain, how your body responds, the directions your eyes first move as they shift about, the sweat that may or may not come out of your pores. Really feel how much energy you spend on this genuinely human thing.

8. comfort *(2 minutes):* As I've said before, soothing has been given a bad rap in our culture. How did we ever come to believe that we could be too old or too strong to need some good-old-fashioned comforting every once in a while?

Cheryl was beside herself with fear when her husband said he was going to give their neighbor flying lessons. The fear made no sense. Her husband was a professional pilot, their neighbor a responsible guy. But Cheryl was still afraid, really afraid. She racked her brain to figure out where this fear was coming from, and why. There was no obvious answer. It didn't even occur to her *not* to figure anything out and just ask for a nice reassuring hug instead. Even big kids need comforting. In this next week seek an opportunity to comfort or be comforted. See how it feels.

9. comfort yourself *(2 minutes):* How do you calm yourself down when something simple happens, like getting angry? Or when something more serious happens, like losing your spouse or job? Some people reach for chocolate. Others pick up the phone and call a friend. Write down your favorite self-calming techniques for both simple disturbances and severe ones. Overachievers, notice if you've made any changes to the way you comfort yourself since you've started this book.

10. when hope is heavy *(1 minute):* Your belief in someone can be the magic ingredient that pulls him or her out of a slump, up a slippery slope, or down the right path. But, paradoxically, holding out hope for someone who isn't *ready, willing, and able (all three!)* to take the next step can be beyond frustrating, and cause a real drain on both of you. Identify someone that you are holding out hope for and try to recognize whether or not, at this moment in time, that hope is a productive thing.

11. go for a spin *(2 minutes):* Many people over seventy years old report that they don't exercise because they have a fear of falling. They may or may not have ever actually fallen before, they are just afraid of it ever happening. Professional dancers, on the other hand, learn to work with the feeling of dizziness instead of fearing it. It's not that they don't get dizzy spinning across a large dance floor, it's that they know that the dizziness will both come—*and go.* Usually after a count of three.

Standing, sitting in a swivel chair, or lying on a carpet or bed (whichever is within your physical skill), spin yourself around at least three times. Notice how dizzy you become and exactly how long the dizziness lasts. Please remember to breathe.

12. your personal dance floor *(1 minute):* As you're reading these words, picture in your mind's eye the size of your personal playground, the territory that you cover in a given day. It certainly includes where you live, and likely includes where you work, travel, go to school, drive your kids to school, where you do your errands, and where you play. Feel your stomping ground. Then with your next breath, with your attention on your heart, ask your body if it likes its current life . . . or if it's secretly yearning for a bigger or smaller dance floor.

13. palla pazza *(as long as you'd like):* The goal of this step is to walk gracefully through life, no matter what situation comes your way, staying yourself more minutes of every day. To become a *palla pazza* (bouncy ball), and spring back from life's falls easily. Below you'll find as many different ways to do this as there are facets to a gemstone. Choose your favorites, and give them a try.

Remember, we're going for realness. No plastered-on smiles, no happy-face masks will work here. We want to budge the bulk, clear the air, fiddle with the frown, lift the heaviness, and nudge the nonsense to let more of the real you come out to really, really, really play. Staying small serves no one. We're on a mission to glow.

- **FIRST THINGS FIRST.** Just as we did in Feel (Step 1), let's start with the basics here. Eat, drink, sleep, pee, and have company in your day. Give your body what it needs to do its job. Power your engines. It'll help you stay real. Sleep deprivation won't!

- **BRUSH IT OFF.** Agnes' father died when their family of eight was still quite young. When the burden on her mother would become particularly heavy, Agnes could feel it in the air, and wondered if her mother was going to crumble under its weight. But to Agnes' delight, it was always at this very point that her normally soft-spoken mother would get a certain determined look in her eye, and with calmness, precision, and vigor, say, *"To hell with it!"* The weight would magically lift off her shoulders, parting the clouds in her internal sky. If the world is going to come crashing down, let it happen *over there.* Try this to see if it lightens your step.

- **STRENGTHEN THE ENERGY CUP.** Think of something or someone that drains energy out of your cup. Choose a real *gusher,* not just a drip, drip, drip. Now, is there a shift that you can make internally (which can be as simple as a choice) to keep all of the energy in that cup of yours, even with that other thing going on?

- **LAUGH IT OFF.** Think back to when you've split your gut laughing. When you laughed so hard it hurt. Not a laugh you had at anyone's expense or one that was under the influence of drugs, tequila, or a few too many beers. We're looking for the authentic belly roar, one that comes from the deepest part of the gut and brings its voice out to infect the world. Overachievers, with that image in mind, see if you can't see the light side of whatever problem you're facing right now.

- **WASH IT OFF.** If noise is on your signal, tension on your shoulders, head straight to the shower, bidet, or tub and wash it right off—physically. If you're in a rush, wash your hands or splash warm water on your face. Overachievers, top it off with some refreshing skin cream.

- **FRESHEN UP.** Change your clothes. Mow the lawn. Repaint the room. Do whatever you feel will freshen up your outlook.

- **TIME IT.** The next time you have a feeling that sends you to the fridge for a comforting nibble, try timing it to see just how just long its discomfort lasts. Seeing the actual number of minutes may put things in a fresh perspective.

- **BRING YOURSELF BACK INTO YOUR BODY.** If you find yourself upset, mind racing out of control, grab your fingers one-by-one and gently pull on them. Perhaps one will call out your name more loudly than the rest. If so, hold it, then breathe fresh air directly from its tip.

- **BREATHE IT OUT.** One good breath can take off even the hardest edge. If you are fighting with someone, however, be careful that your sigh is not misconstrued!

- **TALK IT OUT.** My friend Soleira prefers a talking approach to moving uncomfortable feelings out. "I don't try to get rid of emotions anymore. I express them," she says. "Okay, a little roughly sometimes, I must admit . . . but my housemates know that my point is not to get mad, it's to see what's really underneath." She likes the sense of freedom that she gets, that they *all* get when even the tiniest household tension is cleared from the air on the wings of words.

- **ACT IT OUT.** Beat a pillow, scream at the top of your lungs, rip a telephone book in two. Get tension out of your system with physical movement. Emotions are

See all your choices?

just energy in motion (e-motion). They actually *want* to move. So take advantage of this.

- **WRITE IT OUT, PART ONE.** Try writing an e-mail or letter to someone. It forces you to reason things out more clearly than you may do verbally.

- **WRITE IT OUT, PART TWO.** Write to someone you don't even know, but who inspires you just the same. Ask Neil Armstrong advice on mustering up the courage to go beyond a geographical boundary, Teddy Roosevelt about pulling together a group of people to work for the common good, or Marilyn Monroe what was fun to her about being a woman and what she would do differently if she had it to do all over again. Go wild.

- **MOVE IT OUT.** Whether it's a walk around the block, up Mt. Rainier, or an exercise class at the gym, movement helps clear tension from your body, as well as the air around you. Even five-minute walks help.

- **REPETITIVE MOVEMENTS.** Sometimes people go for drives (with no destination in mind), take showers (when they aren't even dirty), hang their wash out on the line (even if they have dryers), or wash dishes by hand (even if they have dishwashers) just to clear their minds.

- **UPROOT YOURSELF.** Regain perspective by physically breaking away from whatever tension is gripping you. Go across town, state, country, or world for however long you need. Sometimes just going to a great movie or a new neighborhood can do the trick.

- **CHANGE OF AIR.** If you want to approach uprooting from another angle, follow the Italians lead and *cambiare aria,* change your air. See if you can physically feel the difference between mountain, seaside, city, and country air. Breathe it in.

- **SING IT OUT.** Whether in the shower, choir, front yard, or car, belt out your favorite song. At the top of your lungs, with the CD player on "repeat" (that can be really fun), however you'd like, sing for as long as it takes to crack yourself wide open.

- **WIND IT OUT, PART ONE.** If your mind is filled with racing thoughts, instead of trying to stuff them away, beat them at their own game—tire them out. Just let them keep racing, following them down whatever strange paths until you reach the end of their roads.

- **WIND IT OUT, PART TWO.** Sometimes just asking ourselves "What's the worst thing that could happen?" can get us right to the end of the line, bringing us back to our senses and popping any bubble of fear or frustration.

- **SLEEP IT OFF.** Doesn't a good night's sleep change the world sometimes? Put a nice thought as the last one in your mind, and a most pleasant feeling as the last one in your heart, to percolate during dreamtime. Overachievers, for extra relaxation, try showering before going to bed.

- **TAKE A NAP.** Five minutes, five hours, whatever works for you. Take an adult "time out."

- **LET NATURE TAKE ITS COURSE.** Get out into nature—the mountains, sea, backyard, local park. If you're rushed for time, candles can take the place of a roaring bonfire.

- **CHECK IT OUT.** Assuming you know what another person meant can often cause trouble, adding to the uncertainty and noise of your day. Break the silence. Ask for clarification.

- **QUIET DOWN.** Sometimes we complicate things by trying to make ourselves overly clear. My aunt doesn't mind if people misunderstand how or why she does what she does. There are times to make your thoughts

*the options
keep coming.*

very, very clear to one another. And other times that it's just not important. You decide.

- **BREAK IT UP.** Taking things one step at a time breaks down anxiety. Like when unloading the dishwasher seems too hard (or dull), the first step could be to open its door. Then a little while later, you can put the clean dishes on the counter. Then when the energy is just right, take that final plunge and put the dishes away.

- **TURN IT OFF.** If whatever is bugging you has a power switch, save yourself aggravation by turning it off. This means news reports, television shows, radio stations, Internet connections, and telephones. You can get facts without sensationalism and entertain yourself without anxiety.

- **JUST DO IT.** If it's your "to-do" list that's getting you down, it may take less energy to just get it done instead of complaining about not having done it yet, or worrying about whether or not you can complete it successfully. Finish it. Now.

- **JUST DON'T DO IT.** A friend claims that in times of real stress, no decisions should be made after 4:00 P.M. Save them for the freshest hours of the morning.

- **WAIT IT OUT.** Unplug the phone if you know you're too angry to talk rationally. Conversely, if someone else is too angry to be rational (or even a little too tense to be pleasant to be around), politely excuse yourself and leave them alone for a while.

- **POTATOES.** Another friend of mine swears by potatoes—any kind. They calm her right down. Chocolate to pep you up, she says, and potatoes to bring you back down. I'd add a little protein and some complex carbohydrates to the mix to lengthen the tail of your energy and round it out a bit. Others would add calcium, claiming it soothes the nerves. So where does this leave us? With a calcium-packed bowl of ice cream with nuts on top, chocolate sauce, and crumbled-up potato chips drizzled over, with a nice banana on the side. Works for me.

- **VOICE CHANGE.** Artificially change the tone of your voice from agitated to pleasant (or gently ask the angry person in your house to!) and see the effect it has on tension. Clearing the air could be just that simple.

- **BE ALONE.** My cat, Zsa Zsa, would rather be alone than with someone she doesn't like. See if this works for you. Try it—even on a Saturday night!

- **MASSAGE IT AWAY.** Slip away for a massage. If money's an issue, you can often find massage schools that need bodies to practice on—either for free or a minimal charge.

- **STUFF IT AWAY.** You can always revert to your-favorite-good-old-faithful-stuffing technique if you don't feel like dealing with an emotion or two.

- **FAKE IT.** If all else fails and not a single one of these techniques works for you, just pretend you are a person who is clear, stable, and true. And do what you think a person like that would do.

14. be a kid again *(1 minute or more):* If you're lucky enough to have a little one (or two!) nearby, take off the parent-older-sibling-grandparent-family-friend-grown-up hat, get down on the floor or out in the yard, and play, play, play. Follow the kids around, let them lead. Do what they do, every single-strange-absurd-adorable-nonsensical-and-loveable thing.

If no kid is available, pretend you are a kid once again. Imagine you know your way around town by the location of the gumball machines. Look at that tempting pile of leaves that was just raked up, and feel your sadness at seeing it being stuffed into black plastic bags. Marvel at how those silly adults can walk by a cat without petting it. And always expect that friends will come to visit, presents will arrive, and each and every promise made to you will be kept.

15. it's time to finally decide (*one moment*): You have the capacity inside you right now to stay yourself every minute of each and every day. If you choose to, you can realize right now that you are, indeed, safe inside your very own skin. You know what to do. You always have. There is no better place to be. Yesterday has gone. Tomorrow is yet to come. By embracing the power of this very moment, you can handle any experience that life sends your way.

You are more than the car you drive. You're not the sad mood that you are sometimes in. You aren't the names you've been called or the boxes you've been stuffed into. You are more than the friend you lost, the money you found, the promotion you got, or the trouble you're in. You are bigger than the size of your house or skin. You are simply bigger than any of these things. You are a marvelous, vital, passionately alive, perfectly imperfect human being.

You feel big, and it's not at anyone else's expense. You feel in control of life, without the need to control it, yourself, or anyone else. You feel relaxed in the middle of what used to be called stress. You've made the choice, the choice to be as big and beautiful as you were always meant to be. Being the least bit small is a thing of the past. You've made a commitment to living a life that's alive, less whipped around by the whims of the day, one that has you at its core—*ready, willing, and able* to work, serve, and play.

wrap up

You can think of this step as a workout for your soul. And as with all exercise, its goal is to keep you flexible, limber, and light . . . to oil your joints and strengthen your muscles. Lightening up can be playful and fun. It's a good-natured spring breeze, an opening of perspective, the great view you can suddenly see when you round a new bend in the road. By its very nature, lightening up draws breath into your lungs, tickles your heart, stirs your soul, and puts the kind of smile on your face that crinkles the corners of your eyes.

a pregnant pause

There is a natural plateau in this process. You've just reached it. For most of us, myself included, getting here is a big accomplishment—huge, gigantic, insights galore—and it deserves both a hearty celebration and a healthy reflective pause. Think back to how far you've come, how many sensations you've felt, every forward step and stumble. Think about the times you found parts of yourself in the pages of this book, the paragraphs that seemed to be written expressly for you.

Bring into view the complete experience you've had so far, with its good and bad parts, each sporting its own unique voice and perspective. Perhaps your relationship with feeling has shifted a bit, perhaps not. Maybe you are getting a better sense of how emotions move, how they can be viewed as simple energy. Maybe an order to what you previously thought of as chaos is now hinting at you, puzzle pieces fitting together in a slightly different way than they had before. You've done well. Pat yourself on the back, relax, and enjoy your new point of view.

soul maintenance

The care, feeding, and alignment of the soul

STEP 1, FEEL
Come back to your senses.

STEP 2, CLEAN
Clean off who you aren't.

STEP 3, POLISH
Shine up who you are.

STEP 4, WALK
Stay yourself more each day.

the steps in review

we've come a long way

For those of you reading the book from front to back, let's review just how far we've come. For the people who are hopping around, this summary of the first four steps might give you an idea of where you want to go next.

STEP 1, FEEL. We began with brushing off our sensing skills—reawakening our noses, ears, eyes, taste buds, and skin.

STEP 2, CLEAN. Keeping in mind the signal-to-noise ratio, a model for finding ourselves, we used our built-in energy cups to help us distinguish what supports our signals and what adds to the noise of our days. Our spirits became less muffled as we disassembled the activities, people, and stuff that had distracted, suffocated, and cluttered them before.

STEP 3, POLISH. Taking advantage of our newfound lightness, we took a nice long shower and stepped out into the world, discovering more about who we really are, who we connect with, and the things we like to do. We gave ourselves permission to feed off the connections we have with others in a healthy, powerful, and satisfying way—illuminating our shine and starting the flow of our inner glow.

STEP 4, WALK. We learned to pick ourselves up from an annoyance or stumble, dust off, and keep clear, regardless of who or what might be near. We discovered new gears for our inner engines. Perspective, sense of humor, and acceptance played important roles.

If you've been doing the exercises in the first four steps, you've finished a complete pass through the cleaning, sort- ing, selecting, disassembling, and reassembling of your daily routine—and whether you realize it or not, aligned this routine with the desires of your soul. After all, what do you suppose provides the power to fuel life's changes if it's not your soul? What is the force that lifts your spirits when you make a clear, conscious choice? What fills you inside with a feeling of contentment that can't be faked in any way or bought in a store? Of course, it's your soul, truly the most powerful force (and resource) in your possession. And with the proper care and feeding, it can become even more so.

After all, what do you suppose provides the power to fuel life's changes if it's not your soul? What is the force that lifts your spirits when you make a clear, conscious choice?

By aligning with this inner force, you keep more energy in your "energy cup," uncover new harmonics of your "signal," and see more clearly the power of your connections with your friends. And when disharmonious "noise" comes your way, you use your bigger perspective to regain your balance a little more quickly each time. That's huge. Enormous. A really, really, really big deal. So pop the cork, fire off the cannon, strike up the band. And let me be the first to give you a hand.

Because it is within these subtleties that the soul likes to hide, in the smallest changes of our energetic state.

The next four steps take another pass through the same people, activities, and stuff in your life, but from a deeper level, heightening the sensitivity of our familiar energy cups . . . then retiring the cups altogether. We move beyond the energy cup's big energy gains and drains (we don't need those extremes anymore) in favor of the more subtle sensations of openings and closings, contractions and expansions within. We enter a magical realm of direct soul connection—no translators needed.

The tiniest shrinking is of interest to us here. The faintest voice that speaks before our energy cup brings a drop in or out. The softest rounding of the shoulders or caving in of the chest. Why, you ask? Because it is within these subtleties that the soul likes to hide, in the smallest changes of our energetic state. The soul speaks in the moment of transition when we feel open wide to the world, then begin to close down. It whispers through the most minute thought or action that shifts us ever so slightly from that closed-off view and reopens us once again. It winks as it makes us feel bigger, stronger, upright—without the need to put anyone else down. These are soulful moments. These moments contain the mystery and magic of life.

Our goal is, by book's end, to experience fully opening to the wonderful life we already have and to how wonderful a life even more aligned with the soul could possibly be. Our soul is in its glory when we're fully opened. Open is its most powerful place to be.

It's not to say that by the book's end shrinking feelings will go away altogether (they won't), or that it's even the goal that they do (it's not), or that reaching any kind of perfection is our aim (we're genuinely imperfect humans by design, remember?). It's just to say that even the most subtle closures and openings we feel will become quite familiar to us. They are the most direct language that our soul uses. They are whispers (and sometimes shouts!) from the most sacred part of ourselves—clues for our brains, fuel for our engines, and wind for our wings.

When I was writing this book and arrived at the place where you are right now (the end of Step 4) I felt an enormous sense of relief, the "bricks and mortar" part of my work done. I went to sleep content with only one more chapter in my heart to write.

The next day a surge of energy overtook me as I sat down at the keyboard filled with Step 5. A wave of creativity bubbled up from my ocean floor, carrying both me and my laptop with it. On the wave's crest I surfed, painting a picture of life on the other side of the soul-maintenance-oriented world, offering an artistic brushstroke of a less linear, more free-flowing life that is possible. One where push-pulls exist, but passions rule, and long-term inner conflicts aren't allowed. One where each soul is valued, respected, well-tuned, vital, and alive. Twenty-eight pages were born that very crisp fall day, easily twice my previous personal best.

It was a farewell party, parting gift, mind-expanding tease for the reader and playful challenge for me, with a soft, graceful landing for both. *Open your mind, soften your heart, and move with your soul,* I wrote. THE END.

But when my friend Marla read this final chapter of the book, she stated with a certainty that couldn't be ignored, "You're not done yet, Sally. It made me hungry for more."

A huge "*Yes!*" bounded out of me, literally lifting me up and out of my chair. My heart leaped at the thought of focusing its attention on the creative wave that each of us has inside. To find words to express its movements. To give us permission to fly.

Into the wave I dove, the very one that had wet the pages of the old Step 5. I felt into the invigorating surf, joining it on a ride. I could have dissected it analytically, cutting the wave to bite-sized chunks, but that would have killed it, rendering it useless, destroying its power. I strove to keep the wave intact, its momentum alive, and describe its inner workings not by how it looked from the outside, *but by how it felt to a person from within.*

the steps ahead of us

a bird's eye view

Here's a taste of what's to come.

STEP 5, DIVE. We jump straight into our signals, and touch our very souls—vast, fertile, mysterious, immeasurable as an ocean—then splash around a bit. Depending on how well-hidden our souls had been, opening them can feel like a cork popping, a stuck faucet sputtering free, or the graceful rush of fully opening an already free-flowing valve.

STEP 6, FLY. Using the metaphor of a bird in flight, we harness the energy of the "flapping and yakking" that fills a normal day to take flight ourselves. Pain becomes a flying partner, we learn not to shrink from it anymore. We learn, instead, to expand into its contraction, open after we close down, rebound, and enjoy the strength and perspective it brings.

STEP 7, SOAR. We take to the skies with our inner treasures in hand, seeing farther than far, opening wider than wide. The prevailing winds from both our inner passions and the outside world are our guides. When we reach the right altitude, we stop "doing" anything at all, partnering with the pleasure of the experience, letting *it* move *us* for a change.

STEP 8, GLOW. Passion is our partner, bringing us the gift of a hearty visible glow. Truth is our magic wand. People are our fairy godmothers, elves, and friends. We're after one thing and one thing only: a life that's completely, authentically, and wholeheartedly alive.

---

soul movement

Steering life directly from the soul

STEP 5, DIVE
Touch your soul.

STEP 6, FLY
Build your energetic muscles and take flight.

STEP 7, SOAR
Give up the effort and soar with the wind.

STEP 8, GLOW
Partner with your inner passions.

I'd entered a non-linear world beyond intuition to inner creativity. A world where the surface senses are support characters, the heart and soul the leads, and inner passion the star—with the mind the twisted bad-boy, comic relief, and hero all-in-one. A world where each person is both more connected to each other and, paradoxically, more free.

The new Step 5 begins with a conscious stirring of the soul, an acceleration of its velocity. Steps 6 to 8 work with the soul's movements, helping us to recognize its role in our daily lives, showing us how to harness its pulsing rhythms and bring out its passion and drive.

For those of you like Marla, who are ready for seconds, screaming *"Hell, yes!"* from the rooftops, please turn the page.

being alive

alive

1: having life: not dead or inanimate 2: still in existence, force, or operation: ACTIVE <kept hope-> 3: knowing or realizing the existence of: SENSITIVE <-to the danger> 4: marked by alertness, energy, or briskness 5: marked by much life, animation, or activity: SWARMING <streets-with traffic> 6: used as an intensive following the noun <the proudest boy->

Webster's Ninth New Collegiate Dictionary

step 5, dive

GOAL: **TOUCH YOUR SOUL.** *The soul will wait patiently for years, decades even, while you busy yourself with your daily duties, steering your life by tradition, habit, or willpower alone. But when the opening appears, the softening, the inward dive, your soul will stir its great forces to awaken itself—and you. These are the moments that change life as you know it. Every time.*

Welcome to Step 5, the direct soul dive. Grab your snorkel gear and let's begin. First things first: for our souls to open wider than they ever have before, at least initially, we have to slow down and let *them* set the pace. Then, after our soul's inner fires are stoked, we'll be able to coordinate our movements and walk, run, or sprint once again.

As you read the following story of a plane flight I once took, feel into the soul opening that occurred for both the businessman and me. Every turn of events. Each sensation. Even though it looks like it was *his* big moment to burst wide open, moments this powerful are always, always a two-way street. Join us on our flight. Feel the pace that the soul sets, the layered way it moves, the force of its very natural (and often surprising) push-pull. If you're ready, breathe three nice nourishing breaths and begin.

a tale of two souls

The flight crew was preparing to pull away from the gate, reaching to close the cabin doors, as the final passenger rushed in. Since the only empty seat on the plane was the one right next to me, I had a special interest in watching him hurry, flustered and embarrassed, down the aisle. This stranger and I would be sharing at mini-

"Can one really learn to feel again after all these years?" he asked, the tone of his voice, his neatly pursed lips, and formality of his wording communicating more completely than mere words ever could.

mum a physical proximity, and at most a pleasant conversation, over the next couple of hours. Most of the other passengers looked away or down as he moved past. There was the occasional bored sigh from one of them, implying that he'd kept us waiting, although it wasn't really true. It was more that he'd broken the etiquette of business travel, a sacred ritual for the seasoned traveler.

I assumed from his outer appearance that we wouldn't have much in common. He was the quintessential conservative businessman returning to London after a short business trip. He wore a light gray suit, rumpled from the rush, with a light sweat glistening on his brow. A tall, erect, serious stature. Wire-rimmed glasses. Not a pound overweight. A "tight biscuit," as one of my friends would say. When he struck up a conversation, I couldn't have been more surprised.

"I'm headed to a conference," I soon told him.

"Oh, really, on what subject?"

"Bringing a heart to business." Assuming this would send him running, I paused to give him a chance to abort the conversation right there. But he remained interested, genuinely so, though at the time I couldn't be sure. I told him that I was going to be speaking on how to combine the body's innate intelligence with the brain's analytical abilities. "A *think-and-feel* approach to decision-making," I added.

The word "feel" visibly pierced him as if it were a knife, causing him to jerk ever so slightly, as his magic moment began. Time slowed to a near stop, as if at his soul's command. I watched the rhythm of his breath alter, his expression change, his posture tighten, as he gathered himself together, trying to hide his minor transgression and reconcile the force that was stirring inside him. Once again confident in his composure, but barely so, he turned to face me and posed a single question.

"Can one really learn to feel again after all these years?" he asked, the tone of his voice, his neatly pursed lips, and formality of his wording communicating more completely than mere words ever could.

It was another unexpected question, but decidedly genuine this time. It wove the story of his English upbringing, the perfect little boy, born into the perfectly ordered family, trying to find the way to keep even the smallest bit of his real self in there at the same time. He'd surely played the perfect work associate, having found the perfect button-nosed wife, and had the perfect number of perky, intelligent kids who attended the perfect preparatory schools. After one promotion at the job and another, then a third, he'd moved to his present perfect role of corporate vice president.

There was but one lone spot in his eyes that betrayed this ideal, carrying the light of his childhood memories and his long-forgotten dreams. It was a traitor to his professional image, to his traditional integrity. A signal of his inner misery and a flicker of hope rolled into one. Fear surrounded it, one could see, constricting his facial muscles and making it ever-so-slightly more difficult for him to breathe. His impeccable behavior seemed lifeless, his choices predictable. The rules that he'd mastered so long ago formed his present-day prison bars.

But this lone hopeful spot was strong—a fire that refused to die, and a surprise and delight to me. It pleaded to be let out, to be given space to play, room to breathe . . . as his hands remained neatly folded on his lap beneath his monotonously patterned tie and above his perfectly polished shoes.

In the power of that slow-motion magic moment, he found himself wondering (for the first time in years) how he'd let himself get so disconnected. How he'd ended up like this. Just how long had it been since he'd actually felt excitement at seeing his wife and kids? He could remember having felt it once. He could maybe even pinpoint the year when the feeling first began to fade within him, covered by the stress of his duties, his genuine happiness turning into a pretense, an act, another thing to do in his day. It had been these internal questions that had powered his spoken words that day on the plane, that had formed the question for me that had rolled so formally, jarringly, and movingly off his tongue.

Then in a second slow motion moment that immediately followed the first, his eyes formed two tears. Not the eyes that people saw, but the eyes that both he and I felt, the eyes of that single revealing spot, the eyes deep inside.

He and I could both feel the first lie that he'd ever told as it flashed across his mind—nothing big at all, just a little white one, one to make things a little easier, to help him fit in. Then the next lie and the next scrolled through, like on a TV screen. Each had been easier to tell than the one that came before, forming a mask that changed like a chameleon depending on who was around. Word choices were programmed. Facial expressions set. Body gestures coordinated. Opinions held in. Assignments accepted. Choice after choice was made in the name of politeness, security, and success.

No individual decision had seemed particularly harmful, at least not at the time. It was all so slow, so gradual, that he hadn't really noticed how far he'd strayed from who he really was and what he really liked to do.

In a third magical moment much like the previous two, memories of the day before he left on his business trip suddenly filled his mind. The day his boss yelled at him for something and he just sat there, motionless, attentive, the true company man. "I'll take care of it," he'd said, forcing a confident smile to his lips, then adding a coordinated nod to punctuate the effect. He remembered going back to his office and barking at someone out of the frustration of it all, then swearing at himself for how much he'd liked doing it.

Then back in real time, having mentally returned to his airplane seat, the businessman's thoughts suddenly became angry, forming a potent fuel. Imagine how ridiculous, his anger jeered, that there could be a place for a heart in business. That the feeling nature of a human being could fit in a world of politics and promotions. Impossible. Absurd. You'd be crushed if you tried to take down your guard. All hell would break loose. Nothing would get done. Can't this woman next to me see that it could never be so? That you'd be taken advantage of, manipulated, ridiculed? His head tried to rationalize away the ideals as a fourth magical moment appeared, and a river of tears (a sensation he'd not felt in decades) was coming alive in the eyes that both he and I felt, the ones deep inside.

On my side of the interchange, in my inner world, his rigid formality and pleading, authentic look formed new bookends for me, expanding my outlook. Here, in this one man, two extremes were alive. My passion cried out to bring them together—to flip numbness into vitality, desperation into hope. I wanted to show people that when there are more questions than answers, when there is more confusion than not, that it's a time to celebrate, a day to mark on your calendar with a big fat red star. As uncomfortable as it can feel, as out of control as it may seem, your soul is on the move, revving its engines, building the power to change your world.

A soul is a precious thing. It weighs nothing at all, but holds all of our thirsts, hungers, playful wants, heartfelt desires, hopes, and dreams.

In that magical series of moments, as our connection grew, my precious life was forever changed, too. My work opened wider than it had been the day before, a poster-boy found, a new goal formed. I knew that my manuscript would have to be rewritten, new research done, and that my timeline had just slipped out at least another year. Such was the power of that moment's revelation into things that I hadn't yet considered and didn't yet know the answers to.

"Yes," I said as the pregnancy of our individual moments came full-term. "Yes, one *can* learn to feel again after *any* length of time."

With new worlds successfully opened both between and within the two of us, we ended our conversation, exchanged business cards, and turned to our reading, knowing that neither of our lives would ever be quite the same again.

soul food

A soul is a precious thing. It weighs nothing at all, but holds all of our thirsts, hungers, playful wants, heartfelt desires, hopes, and dreams. Its passion has the power to move mountains. But the soul has a timid side, too. One criticism can send it running for cover. A breakup can put a padlock on its door. A failure can erect a barricade. Lies, even little white ones, can form a mortar. Abuse, a fortification . . . better yet, a moat. It's good, right? Protection. Self-defense. Safety. Security. Or is it?

Yes and no. Any form of self-protection is right at the time, by definition, because it's what you need in order to handle what's in front of you. You were likely too small, too scared, too surprised, too puzzled, too inexperienced, too hurt, or too angry to do anything else. But in each life comes a time when it begs for a change, a blossoming, a deeper love, an openness into the new in the largest sense of the word. In these moments, it's an open-hearted partnership with life that our souls seek.

Many things have the potential to stir the soul: a simple flower or sunset, a job loss or break-up, a money windfall, or a baby's birth. Or, as in the case of the English businessman and I, a ten-minute conversation between two strangers on a plane.

But it's equally true that you can meet dozens of strangers, see thousands of flowers, lose or make lots of money, dump and get dumped dozens of times, without even so much as a budge to that great ocean within. Just what is it that turns our light switches on? That sneaks up on us and sends us begging for, demanding, or craving something more? The answer is our willingness, consciously or unconsciously so. Some may call it destiny. Others a choice. But no matter what, like a volcano's eruption or mountain stream's gentle trickle, the moment will arrive, often catching us by surprise with its fervor, and most definitely changing the plans we had for that week, month, year, decade, or day.

This most sacred part of us is patient, strong, and extremely picky. It awaits the proper setting and the right people around to come out. One dose of honesty will send the soul soaring. A measure of true respect, hurl it sky-high. A bit of unwavering belief, and as big as a room we'll become, as invincible as a lion, as light as a sunbeam, and as fluid in our movements as a graceful swan.

An open heart is what we both crave and despise. It's the push-pull of our existence, the undercurrent that draws our attention back to connections that we may be missing, to dreams that we once had, to yearnings that refuse to go away. With hearts safely closed, we wait to win the lottery to be happy, for the next promotion so that we can "get the house, car, and girl." We're sure that money is the answer, that success will be the key.

But what are we really waiting for, I ask? Aren't we just admitting defeat, that we can't be happy with what we have *today?* We've heard this question before, but I'm asking you to *feel* it today. Feel the defeat, the heaviness, the pressure of pushing to get somewhere that you may want to go, but that doesn't really seem to want to be. Of convincing him, of manipulating her, of pushing this, of forcing that, of avoiding the other, or of holding out hope long past its expiration date.

Then feel the triumph, the lightness, and the energy that arrives the moment we open our hearts to the possibility that maybe, just maybe, we are safe, secure, and fulfilled right now, in this moment, with what we have today. With doing nothing more than filling every single cell of our skin and giving ourselves a break for not being somewhere else yet or where someone else wants us to be. Our world *is* in order. All the plans *are* in place.

Can fulfillment be as simple as a choice to invite it in? Certainly, I say, as long as you're connected to what's going on within. Some disassembly is always required—of people, activities, mindsets, and stuff. And you can't pretend anymore that you don't know who, which, or what. You know exactly what's weighing you down, holding you back, draining your energy. It's simply confidence to make a change that we often lack.

The soul is designed to move—itself, the outer you, and everyone around you. It's our engine, our passion, our drive. When we touch it, it sends shivers down our arms, legs, and spines. When we open it up, it comes out of our lips and off our fingertips. And when we trust it to lead the way, look out world! Miracles are here to stay.

The majority of people find it harder to "fake" anything after having played these games. Opinions, orgasms, and smiles insist on a distinct (and typically higher) level of realness before they will come out. Lies, even white ones, become harder and harder to tell. Tones of voice are less easy to falsify. Pretense becomes a four-letter word. General enthusiasm will be strongest when driven from the soul itself. Although pleasing other people is still a pleasant sensation, pleasing yourself is a decidedly more pleasant one, and understood at an intuitive level to be the best path to gratifying others even more.

playing with the push-pull

Remember in the Pregnant Pause when I said "Good job! You've made it! You've won!" Let's go back to that moment again and breathe it in three times through your open heart directly to your soul. First, open your heart, shoulders back, head up, chest wide. Then breathe in . . . and out. Another breath in . . . out. In . . . out. There we are. That's better.

Let's remind ourselves that we're experts at feeling now. If the exercises we're about to do tense us up even a little bit, let's decide right now to play with it rather than shrink from it. Okay?

if any discomfort arises

- **HOLD YOUR INDEX FINGER.** You pick which one. It's the adult equivalent of sucking your thumb. I'm serious here. I'm not fooling around. It's a Jin Shin Jyutsu technique to calm anyone right down.

- **ROCK AROUND THE CLOCK.** Learning from the little ones, rocking back and forth can be very soothing and fun. I prefer the in-the-chair-front-and-back-or-left-to-right rocking motion myself, and do it often, in fact. Others put themselves flat on their backs on the bed or floor, knees up, then move their whole bodies slowly from side-to-side.

- **SCRIBBLE IN THE MARGINS.** Whenever any doubts, anxieties, or fears pop up, no matter how big, small, valid, or ridiculous, write them down. Be specific with the words you use, breaking down big ideas like "impossible" or "I can't" or "never in a million years" to what they really, really mean to you.

let the games begin: This chapter's playground is meant to stimulate, stir, and soften—gently circumnavigating the soul, coaxing, prodding, searching for openings. Since each soul is different, with its own habits, unique masks, and favorite hiding places—and since only that soul itself can decide what it wants to do next—we are indulging it with attention, hosting a party to which we are our only guests. It's both selfish and delicious, a magical carpet ride. So take all the pressure off, keep your index fingers ready, the rocking action going, and a pen at your side.

You'll notice that the format of the exercises for Steps 5 to 8 has changed a bit. There are no time guidelines and the games themselves are often more conceptual. As before, do any or all of the games that call to you in the most positive way. Use the margins to write in. The "pop" of your cork takes a mere instant, but it's an instant that cannot be rushed, cajoled, manipulated, or forced in any way. Right now, your entire job is to play.

section one: warm-up

These warm-ups are meant to soften, open, and limber you up. If you're confused at any point, ask some kids. They'll get it for sure.

1. watch it. Let go of any grip that time has over you. Years ago I turned off my alarm clock, letting myself awaken naturally, except when I had a plane to catch or a particularly early start to my day. Other people take off their watches. Or set the clocks in the house to all the wrong times. Take your pick and for a few hours, days, weeks, or decades, distance yourself from time.

2. the power of silence. Silence is a powerful force. It can both rev up the mind and calm it right down. It can make a conversation uncomfortable or add intimacy to an afternoon. At times garden work can be too slow or too quiet to stand. At other times, silence can be golden. And when silence is lost, it can instantly be found. It's in the place where words fail. The pregnant pause in a well-executed speech. The expectation of that unreturned call. The movie credits that roll after a particularly dramatic film ending. The silent treatment after a particularly loud fight. The silence of the woods in the first morning light, broken by the song of a lone bird. Add 30 seconds of silence to your day right now.

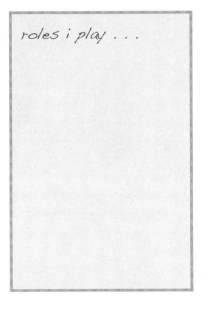

roles i play . . .

3. titles, labels, and identities. Write down every role you currently play—whether "official" or not. Mother, father, worker, manager, student, best friend, devil's advocate, dog walker, cook, housecleaner, bottle-washer, exercise coach, motivational speaker, priest, rabbi, guru.

4. kid stuff. Can you remember one thing as a kid you pretended to like but really didn't? For me it was Donald Duck. Who knows why my mom thought he was my favorite, but I didn't have the courage to tell her the truth. Pretty soon my room was filled with his image—stuffed animals, posters, games, books, knick knacks of every kind. Did you ever get buried alive from one tiny little white lie? Put your awareness in your belly and see if something silly springs to mind.

5. rallentare. I love the Italian word *rallentare*. It means "slow down," something important to do when we're coaxing our souls to come out. Let's start with noticing the natural pace of our breath. Then without trying to make it richer or deeper, simply slow it down. Feel the air moving through your nostrils, turn around, and come back out again. Take another breath, and slow it down even more. Feel any resistance (or pleasure) your body may feel from the slowing of its breath. Then feel how that resistance (or pleasure) reduces (or grows) as your next breath is taken. When you feel satisfied, move on to the next exercise.

6. what's the rush? Are you an hour late for a dinner party? Are you thirty-five and still living at home? No problem in Italy! There's absolutely no rush there, except on the roads.

Have you ever noticed that rushing usually backfires? Locks, computers, and copy machines will often jam when we're in a rush. Where are you rushing your life? Is it working? Remember, this isn't a thinking exercise, it's a *feeling* thing.

7. movement is mandatory. Take three laps around the room, each one at half the pace of the one before. Feel your way, noticing any sensations that arise. Overachievers, take one more lap at whatever pace you'd like, this time focusing on relaxing your stride, loosening your grip, and making more room for your heart in your chest.

8. softness. Locate the softest thing within arm's reach and touch it. It could be fabric, the squooshiness of a laptop  screen, the couch upholstery, your naked baby, a stuffed animal, the cat, or your own body itself. Yes, breasts and bellies count, as does that delicate skin on the inside crease of your elbow. Or that oh-so-soft-and-sometimes-sagging skin under your chin. Reach out and touch it! Search for the softness.

9. look yourself straight in the eye. Go to the nearest mirror and look into your eyes. What colors are they? When you smile, does the skin around your eyes crinkle? Overachievers, look into the eyes of someone else, even your pet. Describe what you see.

10. take a break. You've been working hard. Yes, even these simple warm-ups have started to stir things up. Take a breath in, then let it out. Stretch your arms up over your head. Burp if you want to. Everyone, top yourself off with a nice, relaxing yawn. Relax. You deserve it.

section two: stir the soul

Let's dive right in, from six different angles, and playfully, lightly, gently, poke around our souls and see what treasures we find. Do any or all of the games that call *you* by name.

1. gradual openings. Think back to the story that I opened this chapter with—the English businessman who'd buried himself alive. White lie after white lie he'd told himself and his friends. Sure, he'd like to do this, he'd said. Yes, he'd be happy to do that. But he really wasn't happy at all. In fact, he'd become more disconnected from himself with each seemingly trivial white lie that he'd told.

Let's do the exact opposite and *rediscover* ourselves one small step at a time. This may sound simple, it may sound cliché, but do one teeny tiny nice thing for yourself every single day. Not for a week, not for two. Do it for years. And start today.

The power of this opening is in the initial choice that you make, the choice to serve yourself and to treat this self with kindness and respect. Whether it's a different color eye shadow or a new seat cover for your car, a twenty-minute workout or a three-hour museum tour, a ten-second sip of espresso or a forty-five-minute pedicure, a flower for your garden or freshly washed hair . . . each step will lead you one step closer to the real you. With consistency and practice, your tastes will blossom and change. Step-by-step, day-by-day, you'll unfold into yourself.

Make your choices spontaneously . . . or write a full-page list of the simplest things you can think of that would feel refreshing to you. Be simple. Be creative. Play. Overachievers, think *big*.

little things that feel good . . .

fill that page!

2. magic moments. Whether it be on top of a mountain or in your own living room, magic moments come to us to stir our souls, to show us that there's more to life than can fit in a brain, be captured in a book, or meet an eye. Magic moments make you laugh. They make you cry. They take your breath away. Have you had a magic moment?

When I was a little girl, I had a favorite plant in a little brown-and-white-speckled pot. I can still remember it. Once as I was looking at its light-green new growth, the idea occurred to me that its succulent little leaves would look wonderful with tiny white flowers on them. How I was filled with that sensation, the idea that that might one day come true!

To my delight and surprise, the very next day it did. Small white flowers appeared on every delicate branch. But when I ran to my mom, filled with more magic than on Christmas morn, the confused look on her face suggested that I'd imagined the whole thing.

Lauren and her dad had a magic moment one day. She was about six or seven at the time, and the two of them were playing guessing games. Her father, good manager that he was, wanted to teach her about statistical laws. He asked her to guess a number he had in mind between one and one hundred. She did, "seventeen." And she was right.

"No," he said, "that's not the way you play." He wanted her to divide the problem down to make it easier for herself, conveniently ignoring the fact that the game was pretty easy for her as it was. "You're supposed to ask me, for example, is it between fifty and one hundred? If yes, then between seventy-five and one hundred? And so on . . . " But she continued as she'd been doing before. And she was right on the first guess about seventy percent of the time.

Magic moments are when you feel connected, expansive, in tune with the world. For me, it was when a snow drift made it all the way up to the second story window and we slid down it. Or the day I met my very best junior high school friend. Or when I went on a tour of potential colleges, and knew with certainty which one was right for me. Sunrise at 12,500 feet on my way to the summit of Mt. Rainier. Three solid weeks of non-stop laughter as I was traveling with friends in Africa. The night we spent at the 18,500-foot summit camp of Mt. Kilimanjaro, when I, sick from the altitude, finally fell asleep between two of our African guides. The moment I knew I was pregnant.

Make a list of your magic moments. It may be just one precious event or enough to fill an entire book. Have fun. And remember, there's no rush at all.

magic moments . . .

3. tough times. These moments are the opposite of the pleasant ones we've been discussing, though they may happen to you for good reasons—to force you to face up to something, for example. The ground suddenly moves out from underneath you, making you question everything you thought of as true. Something that worked yesterday doesn't work today. Masks that fit for years are suddenly the wrong shape or size. Longstanding numbing techniques don't satisfy anymore. The chameleon act falls flat, you run out of steam to play one role with this person and another role with that. Maybe your house doesn't even feel like yours anymore. Or your city. Or your job. Friends can annoy you more than comfort you. A sudden rage can boil up. You can feel stagnant. Confused. Lost. Alone.

And if this isn't bad enough, tough times like these can hang around for a long time—hours if you're lucky, or days, weeks, or years.

In my CFS days, my dark period lasted a little over a year as I fought, clawed, and struggled to get back the life that I'd known, not realizing yet that my better option was to embrace my new one. A mother of three had a brief dark moment, a sudden sensation that if she didn't find a way to express herself, to do something just for her, she'd die. A psychologist recalls a period in his early twenties when understanding the meaning of life began to consume him, forcing him to question every decision he made. A woman in her late thirties, during the final stages of a break-up, spoke of her exhaustion—"I'm so tired. So tired of fighting this battle."

These moments, although dressed in black, are but another brilliant facet of the human gemstone. Still, it's hard to say "hooray" when they arrive. It's easier to get sucked into them, to lose both yourself and your perspective. But with a bigger point of view firmly in place, one could just as easily embrace the changes they hold.

When we resist change, we often reason to ourselves that even though we don't really like where we are, in a strange way it's comfortable. At least we know what to do in this place, we know how to be. But perhaps we should consider that on the other side of a thin veil, barely out of reach, something new is waiting for us. And if we're open (that's key!), we can always, always, always find someone to help us step into it.

For this exercise, if you are going through a tough time right now, write down the name of one person *who is willing to hold out a hand without jumping into your pit*. It's a lighthouse that we seek, a stable reference point, not someone who'll go up and down on our wild ride. Overachievers, identify three. And if you can't think of anyone like this, open to the possibility that one day soon, you will.

Confidence, not compassion, is what we want here. Directness versus sugar coating one single thing. Yes, their hearts must be in the right place, their intention to help clear. But their clarity of purpose, their broader perspective, their position on the other side of that veil is what will serve us— *not* their sympathy. You've had enough pity, you've made enough complaints. If it's a real breakthrough that you want, reach out firmly, boldly, and immediately to the person on the tip top of your list. And really, really, really mean it. Make the choice count, even if it sends you shaking from the top of your head to the tip of your toes.

That said, if for some reason, you are not ready today (or if you don't have a human lighthouse nearby), that's okay, too. Just keep on the lookout for the day that you are (or do). I guarantee that the day will come. Your only job is to get very, very, very clear. Take your time, take care of yourself, and keep circumnavigating that magic, immeasurable soul.

4. personal magnetism. My grandmother died a while back. In her preparations, in addition to the box that she put on her guest bed marked "funeral" with her favorite purple paisley dress, pair of panty hose, and best wig in it, she'd taken great pains to empty her house of its contents, finding just the right home for each and every thing.

"It's a pity," she'd said. "I've watched most of my friends die. And their things just get thrown away. Entire lifetimes gone by."

Each time I visited, the house would be more and more bare. What remained was marked with the name of a relative to whom it would be sent after her parting. In the end, her bedroom was the only room left intact. Her favorite framed photos hung on the walls, though the drawers of the dresser had long been cleared out.

It struck me that people have a magnetism that attracts certain people, activities, and things to them. The loss of a person both leaves a sadness in friends' hearts . . . and liberates the collection of knick-knacks, furniture, and stuff that made up his or her home. That same stuff would not make sense to any other living soul.

Sometimes we need films like *It's a Wonderful Life* to remind us that even the simplest life is magical in its own way. That there is a vital quality to each and every human being. In this exercise, let's search for our own. Take a few minutes right now to look around your room. See if you can catch that inner sparkle, that soul's glow, the "you" around which your life turns. Notice the way your choices are different from any other person's. Sense the force that's uniquely yours.

5. direct soul dive. We are going to do a reading meditation. If you're ready to begin, as you read these words, take off any imaginary hats that you are wearing, any roles that you like to play, and let your mind be a little more free. Feel it soften, loosen, then expand to the size of the room. Next, turn your attention to your heart. Put your shoulders back, head up, and chest wide. Breathe in . . . and out, picturing your heart opening wide. Another breath in . . . and out. In . . . and out. There we are.

Riding on the wings of your imagination, as you are reading these words, feel your hand's contact with the book's pages, the touch of your very own skin upon the paper. Bring your awareness to your fingertips, the fullness of their flesh, the aliveness of the skin. Its suppleness or dryness. Whether you've put lotion on it recently or not.

Now, move your awareness to the skin over your entire body, and continue to breathe. Notice how your skin brushes, touches, or presses against the clothes you have put it in. The way any tightness or wrinkles feel from the inside out. Is the skin on your neck different from the skin on your belly? Your ankle from your big toe? Now take another big breath in, feeling your body as a whole. Stay here for a moment, soaking your wholeness in.

If you are ready, dive a little more deeply with me now and feel the you that is more than your skin. You are bigger than any organ, you are more than any one thing. You are more than the car that you drive or the house you live in. You are more than your habits, your clothing, or your things. You are not your title, your lack of one, or the diamonds you may or may not have in your rings. You are more than the kids that you have, if you have them, and you are bigger than any fear you might face. You are more than your parents, your bosses, and your bills. You are more than your moods, dust bunnies, and ills.

You are the glue that holds you together. Without you the collection of people, things, and activities you surround yourself with simply wouldn't exist.

Breathe into your heart and open yourself wide. Give yourself in this moment right now more room to breathe, more space to expand, and more freedom to be your full self. Feel yourself opening like a flower, your passion rising up, bursting out of your heart into the air that surrounds you . . . then breathe this passion back in. Stay with this sensation, the new life replacing the old, until you feel renewed, refreshed, and alive. And know that your soul is a source of passionate power.

Now let's leave our inner world and move to our daily routine. As you read this, continue to breathe in vitality from the air. Breathe into the silence between the notes that you sing, the pauses, however brief, between the words you utter from your lips or type on a page. Breathe into the oil that you use to grease the wheels of your day.

You are the whiteness of your page, the energy of your breath, the tension of your attraction. You exist in the space between each breath, the moment where a contraction turns into an expansion. You are the force that holds your life together. You are a unique voice in the world. Sit for a moment with your imagination, warmth, confidence, and curiosity as your companions. Then, when you're ready, and if you really, really want to, with a simple thought, a playful pretending, expand yourself to fill more than your skin. Fill the room, the building, the universe, and beyond. Effortlessly.

6. touchdown. As our final soul-stirring exercise, let's go past the details and head straight for the goal line to complete the pass of passes, a real touchdown. Have you ever met anyone who immediately, instantly, knew you better than you'd known yourself?

I've been lucky. It's happened to me three times. Even when I'd looked in the mirror and seen only warts, bumps, and bulges, these three older women were unwavering in their confidence, steadfast in their hunches, and firm in their beliefs. They were beyond lighthouses; they were solid as rocks. Even the roughest storms that I'd found myself in couldn't send them away. At first I was confused, perplexed, wondering just what it was that they'd seen. What I'd done to warrant such faith and esteem. In truth, I'd done absolutely nothing at all. They were just able to see around my worries, under my masks, directly to the force that is me.

Being with these women was a sensation like a completed pass, a goal made, a connection complete—*on steroids*. Because I didn't have to even toss a ball out there. I didn't have to do one single thing.

Have you ever met a person like this? Whose confidence in you both stirs your soul and confounds your brain? It could have been a man or a woman. A teacher, relative, doctor, or childhood friend. Or a complete stranger whose reaction you discounted because it made no sense to you then. Please let it make sense to you now. Let that sensation in. Let that first impression get past your head, into your heart, and under your skin. Help yourself to yourself, to those magnificent selves that they saw, right now.

section three: cool down

These exercises are best done quickly, all in a row.

1. movement is mandatory. A magazine ad for a high tech material used to make golf balls described the material as "soft, flexible, rubbery," with the elasticity to absorb more energy from a swing. It minimizes both distracting vibrations and noise, so it's easier for you to hit the ball farther, to go the full distance. Pretend you are made of this high tech material. In whatever position you are right now, make yourself more "soft, flexible, rubbery."

2. open. In this moment, decide that today will not have any limits on it. It will not be constrained to be the day that you thought it would be. Open. Now.

3. put your heart in it. Hold your head up, shoulders back, chest wide, heart open. Pretend that you are diving into your heart, then feel the splash as you hit the river's currents below, the river of your vitality. Ride that river through the rapids to the still waters beneath. Let your imagination guide you to the mouth of this river, to where the soul's ocean kisses it on the other side. Play in the waves until you feel like diving straight in. Ride on the fin of a dolphin straight to the ocean floor. Find the spring that's the source of your vitality. Play with its bubbles, letting them tingle on your skin. Feel them refresh every cell of your being. Then let them carry you up, up, up, and out . . . to the very air that you breathe. Then spend the next few moments breathing that vital energy back in.

4. human touch. Let's indulge ourselves in that one simple word: touch. Feel, rather than think, about the following. And feel free to physically move as it moves you.

- A comforting touch
- The touch of a fly landing on your arm . . . or nose
- A touch around the outside of one ear
- A long-yearned-for first touch
- A wet sticky touch of a child's hand
- A ticklish touch
- A gingerly touch
- A healing touch
- That final touch that you put on something or someone before it goes out the door

5. tentative touch. Have you ever noticed that when you are in a fight, you may both shrug from a touch and desperately want to be touched at the same time?

6. truth serum. My Italian friend Elisabetta almost starved one summer by being too polite. You see, the Italians are the first to tell you *"non fare i complimenti!"* (don't be shy!) when they are serving you food. But they are the same ones that have this oh-so-polite-back-and-forth game of saying "No, thank you" to second helpings. Then the host is supposed to insist on it, and the guest is supposed to refuse once again. Finally, the host insists a second time, and then no matter how animated the refusal, the host puts that extra portion on the guest's plate just the same. It's a cultural script.

But when Elisabetta went to stay with an English family for a summer to improve her language, and said no to seconds of the meat, the host replied, "Okay," and took the plate back to the kitchen. Try as she might, she found it really hard to break this simple habit.

Is there a polite habit you have that is leaving you a little less than satisfied? That's starving part of your life a bit?

7. space. I remember a cartoon where an announcer was interviewing animals in the zoo. When he got to the big cat (a lioness lounging on a tree branch, as I recall), the cat started off with a polite comment or two about how well she was treated. She didn't even have to bother to hunt for her food, she said. But then she added, looking carefully to see how her comment was being received, *"If I could ask for one tiny thing, I'd like some more SPACE. Some room to run. So I could catch some animals—myself. Yes, I'd like more SPACE . . . I really would."* Then her voice trailed off, polite shyness returned, and her eyes turned away from the camera.

That scene has always stuck with me. The cat's outward formality, contrasted with the raw emotion of how she felt inside. The fact that the easy life wasn't always the most satisfying one. Does anything about this cartoon ring a bell with you?

8. more space. As a final exercise for this step, let's create our own space for new possibilities.

- **WANT A PARTNER?** Clear out half the closet and empty some drawers for his or her things.
- **WANT MORE MONEY?** Open a new account, make room for the new.
- **WANT MORE TIME?** Cancel any activity that leaves you the least bit flat. Or start a project that makes your heart sing—right now, today. Create the time, even ten minutes' worth.
- **WANT MORE FOCUS?** For twenty-four hours, do just one thing at a time, giving each activity a little more space. No cell phones while driving. No busywork while having a conversation. Pick one thing at a time, and do it.
- **WANT A SURPRISE?** Leave a weekend entirely unplanned.

wrap-up

The soul, an undeniably powerful force, flourishes on gentleness—soft light to shine on it, plenty of room to move, space to breathe, and time to decide what it wants to do next. When we open to it, it will begin to speak. Even when we hide from it, it will often find a way to get through to our ears.

In my case, my soul rode on an illness to get my attention, sending its messages to me when it knew that I was listening, timing itself with the flaring of my symptoms, something I wouldn't dare ignore. At first, I heard only the symptoms and followed their movements, assuming they were the voices meant for me. Then one day, I distinguished a little voice that spoke the split second before my symptoms made their move, so patient in its efforts, so consistent in its attempts. It was the voice of my soul speaking directly to me.

In this book, we connect deeply inside . . . then pull ourselves way, way out to see how each inner sensation forms a piece of a bigger picture, a natural part of human life, a dynamic of the soul's movement. As a writer might say, it's like living in the "first person" and "third person" at the very same time. Being fully alive and engaged in our world and objective about it, all at once. It gives us power. It sets us free.

step 6, fly

GOAL: BUILD YOUR ENERGETIC MUSCLES AND TAKE FLIGHT. *In this step we discover our subtle magic moments, those tiniest tensions and innermost urges that are the voices of our souls. We learn to listen to those voices and resist shrinking from them—or from anything. Aligning with our souls, we lift on their warm currents and flap our wings to take flight.*

It's easy to see why some people would rather stay put in a cozy nest than fly. It feels safe and secure to know exactly how much money you have in the bank, and precisely what's going to happen each day. But that's only an illusion of safety, if you ask me. An illusion of control over the organic, unpredictable, and changeable thing we call life. If we choose to live controlled, planned, mechanical lives, wings closed up tight, we're missing out on the magic that makes life truly spectacular. And we'll never experience the joy of our soul's inner flight.

Wouldn't you prefer the type of control that comes from well-coordinated, flexible movement? From choosing your pace moment by moment, from deciding whether to walk or to sprint. From building endurance, agility, and strength. From connecting with your truest desires, feeling them rise up from inside, then riding high on their lift.

Wouldn't you prefer to live, breathe, and fly from the very heart of your passions? I would. I can't think of anything else I'd rather do, any place I'd rather be, or any life I'd rather be living—period.

Sure, you have to be willing to endure the occasional toe stub or stumble, emotional gut punch, or rush of fear that can come from taking a big fat risk. You may even have to be willing to shrink in the face of a person who doubts you. And you definitely need to be willing to stay with a tough moment and see it through to its natural end, trusting that you will bounce back with the resilience that comes from a very well-trained set of wings.

Imagine for a moment a bird in full flight. Then imagine that the bird was able to flap its wings only an inch or two—not much strength in that, right? In human terms, it would be the rough equivalent of someone facing an obstacle and then immediately trying to run from it, stuff it back down, fix it, or make it go away. Imagine, instead, if we humans mimicked our feathered friends and endured these contractions for just a little longer, waiting for them to peak before reversing our wing movement once again. Learning to do that would give us strength and control over just about anything.

In this chapter I invite you to become thrilled by the discomfort of stepping out of your comfort zone, and feeling the lift that it brings to even your most routine day. There is such satisfaction in knowing that in those moments when your personal towers are crumbling, when you feel lost, in limbo, empty, alone, and hopeless inside, when your world has been changed or you've hit a dead end, that you have the power to turn it all around, that you have the wings to fly.

ready, set, *contract!*

In order to fly, we have to sense the subtle winds both within and around us, and be comfortable flapping our wings. In human terms this feels like a series of "contractions" and "expansions," punctuated by big and little turning points in between—contract, expand, contract, expand . . . *fly.* Don't worry if this doesn't make sense to you just yet, it's something you have to experience to understand. And lest you confuse flying with work, let me put that myth to rest right now. What's decidedly *more* uncomfortable (and such a waste) is the energy spent resisting, fighting, avoiding, and hiding . . . breathing unclear air, playing it safe. When we fly on our soul's wings, we expand our choices. Our flexibility improves. Mistakes are felt, admitted, then corrected, not held as life sentences.

Let's take the next few minutes to simulate a quick inner flight so you can feel what I mean. In each of the examples below we are presented with a slightly sticky situation, as well as an opportunity to turn it around. See if you can feel the moment of choice.

Pretend you're in school again and the teacher asks a question about something you're interested in. You want to put your hand up, but you hesitate instead. Predictably, the class brain jumps in and you feel yourself shrinking back . . . but your opening appears when he or she gets the answer wrong. Again your hand goes up, your heart leaps high, and you get the answer right.

Now, let's take our flight to the highway. You're in a rush. You cut someone off. You curse and make a nasty gesture or two. A few moments later, you catch yourself, perhaps after taking a breath. At the next light, you let someone in, deciding to give your rushing a brief rest.

Flying is all about a flip of perspective, a powerful softening, a lessening of resistance to any place life may take us.

In a conversation that night, you contract once again by cutting someone off mid-sentence. But this time you notice right away, and take the chance to flip things around and ask an open-ended question instead. The other person smiles and responds eagerly.

Before going to bed, you turn on the TV, hoping to catch the news of the day. The newscaster is fixated, as usual, on one small unpleasant happening, so you press the off button on the remote, choosing not to let yourself dissolve into the bad news.

At the office the next day, you prepare to enter your boss's office. Well-dressed outside, you're shrinking within, as you begin to present your plan for an improvement. *Why are you shrinking?* you feel yourself ask. The answer that rises up is just as surprising. You're shrinking because the ideas that you wrote are too safe, boring, and confining. So instead of presenting your well-polished report, you brainstorm with your boss. The whiteboard is soon filled with scribbles and notes—fresh, creative ideas. You feel your energy rising.

We just took a simple flight. Did you feel the movement? Did you notice that embedded within the smallest shrinking sensation there is always a choice? A choice to use a contraction as a springboard for launching something fresh and new?

You see, souls want to move, to lift us, to soar. We feel a reaction rising up, catch hold of it, notice its predictability, its dustiness, and then choose to respond in a fresher way. We feel an anger rising, and realize that we don't have to carry it around for the whole day, that even the darkest moods can move up and out of our way. We feel a wave of love for our child and let it fill us deliciously. That's soul movement. As souls move, tensions relax. Exaggerations soften. Our base of energy builds. Tasks are cut down to size, the essential steps identified, a synchronistic pace found.

Soul movement is often so subtle that it's only when you look back over a several-month span that you can see the power that built up through your series of big, small, and at times seemingly insignificant, daily choices.

contract, expand, *fly!*

I suppose some of you are still wondering how contracting can possibly be a good thing. You may even think I'm crazy, that I've finally flipped my lid. Indeed, I have . . . and you will, too. Flying is all about a *flip* of perspective, a powerful softening, a lessening of resistance to any place life may take us. Softening with strength. Contracting with courage. Understanding the wonderful paradox that you can't spread your wings wide without pulling them in first.

Picture once again the movement that birds make to take flight. First they contract in (shrink, if you will), then they re-expand their wings out. It's a contraction followed by an expansion. An opening after a close. For flight to take place, birds need to close, open, close, open, close, open . . . *fly*. That's how muscles grow and become stronger. A confidence takes hold. Birds naturally embrace and befriend the surrounding elements. As their altitude climbs, they assume a fully-open stance—and soar effortlessly above the noise.

Close, open, close, open, close, open . . . *fly*. It's the action of a pumping heart bringing fluids to each cell of a body. The contractions of a birth canal. The tapping of your foot. The beat of a bass drum. The movement of your breath. The voice of your soul finding its way up and out, fearless, brought to powerful three-dimensional life.

Believe it or not, most of us already know how to fly. Just think back to your first crush. Chances are good that your feet were nowhere near the ground. You may even remember the details of your particular flight pattern, the way love filled you and made you feel inside. The "wow, look at him or her!" expansion, followed by the "oh, no, she's going out with someone else" contraction that tossed you around in its wake. The "do you think he really likes me?" opening, followed by the "I'm not sure" shrink back, then tossed away just as quickly by the "look at how lovely she is, I sure *hope* she likes me" floating sensation. Whether you get the gal or guy or not, fresh energy rushes to you just the same.

As your heart lifts, it opens, expanding its energy out, giving you the sensation of being lighter, taller, and bigger than you'd been the moment before. You're more flexible as a result. Open-minded. Expansive. Able to see different points of view. You feel good about yourself and your place in the world, and the world feels good about you. On the current of love, your altitude climbs. Contract, expand, contract, expand . . . *fly.*

It's easy to fly on the wings of love, on the breeze of idealism, on the sparkling gust of a new romance. But what about the windstorms or rain showers that life periodically sends our way? When our heart shrinks back in disappointment, annoyance, sadness, or fear, and pulls our body with it, hunching our shoulders, dropping our head. Our energy thickens. Our legs, arms, and chest feel like lead. We contract in, shrink back, hold tight, deflate. Our opinions get rigid. Options disappear. Brightly colored perceptions and visions turn to dull shades of gray. Is it possible to fly under conditions like this? Yes, of course it is—using your own built-in personal guidance system.

Flying is about choice; it's an energetic state that has more to do with perspective than results. Each flap of your wings, each reopening after a contraction, serves as a bellows, fanning your glow's flame. Your glow comes from you being you, regardless of how much comfort—*or conflict*—is in the air.

twists and turns

Initially, it was the hurt from my divorce that spurred me to take jazz dance classes after a decade's absence. But it was the fun of dancing that kept me going every week. I loved the rhythm, the movement, the new friends I made. I would leave class literally singing, a flower in full bloom.

One day as I was driving home from class, I was overcome by a powerful contraction, a sudden feeling of loneliness and despair. It was like my newfound flexibility and openness had shaken something loose. I didn't like it one bit, so I stuffed it right back down, telling the feeling that it had no part in my life, that I didn't want it around. But each and every time I left my dance class, around the exact same bend in the road, the feeling would return with its precise vigor and tone. Then like clockwork, I would shove it back down again, quite happy with myself for my efficiency.

For months I continued like this, until someone suggested that I hang with the feeling a bit more before I sent it on its way. I thought she was crazy. "I have a system that works," I told her. "Why in the world would I want to subject myself to *more pain?*"

"Just a little more," she said. "Then see what happens."

The next time I hit that infamous curve, the feeling arrived and my experiment began. I was shocked when the loneliness and despair lasted *just one split second* beyond the point where I usually stuffed them back down. I'd found my contraction's natural turning point, I now see. A burst of happiness and relief then followed like an internal fireworks show. All those long months the feeling had just wanted to

finish its sentence. How much energy I'd spent stuffing it down instead of simply listening! Thinking back, I never did put words to what it was trying to say. Sometimes words just don't matter.

And sometimes they do. Our souls love when we express feelings with words.

Under grumpiness, for example, could be a physical hunger, our blood sugar could have dropped. Or it could be something metaphoric, a general dissatisfaction with life. If it's the latter, it's your soul speaking. When you put words to what it's trying to say, you can feel the lift from the air that you've cleared, and more often than not, a path out will appear.

Let's take an example. Say it's the family toothpaste tube under attack. Use the tension as a trigger and ask yourself *"What's really going on here?"* Is the person who's angry at your bad squeezing technique tired of cleaning up after you, not just in the bathroom, but in other areas, too? Perhaps there are some other messes around like old arguments, unkept promises, or a crusted coffee cup or two. When the insight arrives, you'll feel its truth.

Perhaps you feel tired a lot. It might be purely physical, a result of too much stuffed into one thin day. Or it could be soulful, signifying that you're tired of something you've been doing. Once again, putting words to what's draining your energy and widening your perspective can be the first steps to sending a block on its way. Then you can ride the lift and enjoy the fresh air.

Let's say there's a dirty diaper to change—no big deal, right? You've done hundreds before. But this time you're particularly tired and that darned stuff is squooshing out the sides. What a mess! Then some little thing turns you around—maybe it's your baby's smile, her eyes, or maybe that cute little bottom, so soft and round. Or maybe something bigger, a reminder that this newborn phase lasts but a short time in what will (hopefully) be a very long life. Then with a clean diaper in place, the snaps of the shirt fastened, both of you are refreshed once again. A tickle or two seals your happiness.

Flying has us harnessing the power of even the toughest emotional waves, turning them into friends. Choosing to do this pops us out of the chaos, the turmoil, the abyss . . . and invites waves of pure inspiration to come rolling in.

partnering with pain

Every time we choose to shrink from our inner urges, whatever they are, we are resisting something. We are holding the truth inside, closing our mouths and hearts, stressing our bodies—until our cork finally pops from the pressure, and we shout the truth at someone. Or kick the family pet. Wouldn't it be better to simply ask ourselves what's really going on underneath the tension instead?

When I was general manager of that factory, we had our share of tense experiences. One quarter, in particular, was an unmitigated disaster, more than half of our shipments were at stake. We were plummeting downward—*fast.* And as if things weren't bad enough, one morning I found on my desk a letter of resignation from the vice president of operations.

It's not that he didn't have a good reason for leaving. He had gotten a great new job where the grass was very green—so green, in fact, that a counter offer seemed futile. Our president, board, and executive team didn't think that we had the slightest chance of keeping him. But my nagging inner voice operated below logic and was sure that he would stay.

And stay Mark did, but only after we got under the annoyance, beyond the frustration, to what was really, really, really going on. Only then was forward movement possible. I suspect that without being faced with Mark's potential resignation (and anger), we might not have gotten our production lines running again so soon. Our pace quickened when each department took responsibility for part of the solution, instead of Mark's team trying to drive the whole thing.

Next, it was my turn to take the hot seat. I was negotiating with our customers over our cost overruns when my cork blew sky-high. I went beyond angry to seething. I was livid. Furious. Out of control. I blew up at one meeting and almost walked out of the next, much to the amazement of our customers and our corporate controller, Chris.

What was under this anger? What wanted to be said? It wasn't only the bottom line that I was fighting for, the dollars and cents. I wanted our customers to show some appreciation for our efforts, as well. And underneath that layer, with a force that I could barely control, was the part of me that wanted payment for *all the times* that people like Mark and I had shouldered responsibility for others, had cleaned up someone else's mess.

The sheer fury of my outburst surprised me. I felt naked and exposed. I was embarrassed at my behavior and honestly afraid of what I might do next. So in the safety of my home, I decided to face my rage directly. I put on some music and sat down.

Contract, expand, allow the tension, feel the release . . . fly.

Immediately, I could feel my belly start to churn, which, according to my mind-body guide, signified injustice, unfairness. That seemed about right. My shoulders began to ache, signifying a resentment over the burdens that I'd been carrying. I breathed into the tingling sensations and, by communicating with them directly like this, lifted both their energy and mine.

I'd ridden my anger up . . . and out. A gentle warmth filled me, restored my perspective, and flipped my cup from half-empty to half-full once again.

The next day I asked Chris to lead the rest of the negotiations. He was thrilled at the chance, and my customers were pleased to see that the usual smile had returned to my face. We all won that day. Contract, expand, allow the tension, feel the release . . . *fly.*

A little while later I received another resignation letter, but this time the person was leaving out of strength, not anger, and I wouldn't have dreamed of stopping her. Over the previous months, her job definition had been changing (along with our business) to something that didn't suit her anymore. I had noticed this earlier and tried to find something suitable within our company, but no such position existed. She needed to look outside (leave the nest, so to speak) which she reluctantly did—then found the perfect fit.

So did we. One person was moved into her vacated spot, which made room for another to transfer to his newly-vacated spot, and a third to move as well. Each of these transfers was directly in line with the gifts and goals of the individuals involved. Contract, expand . . . *fly*.

That's what happens when we work with our emotions and feel our way through the contracting and expanding. We fly.

using the end of my rope as a swing

silly sally

Whether it's a natural disaster we are facing or one made by our own human hands, there are many ways to turn a shrinking feeling around and regain our footing. One option that I discovered quite by accident is that by riding even an enormous contraction to the end of its line, it springs back naturally.

Forza! as the Italians would say. *Strength!*

It was September 11, 2001. I was in Sicily at the time, lost in a sea of fear larger than the Mediterranean, certain that the end of the world was in sight, at least my little world anyway. My brain galloped at the speed of the spirited thoroughbred that I can sometimes be, figuring out every detail of how I could possibly hide in my small apartment for the rest of my natural days.

Like a good Italian, my thoughts immediately turned to my supply of food. I already had some extra pasta. Should I add beans and rice? How about sugar and flour? Then tomato sauce popped to mind . . . and water, yes, water. I added that to my mental list. Canned vegetables, too, because if the worst were to happen fresh ones wouldn't be found. Sugar and coffee, I'd need those, for sure. And back to the water, how could I store enough? Just how much would I need? As the list compiled in my head, my wings closed in toward my chest, triggering a fresh split-second choice.

Part of me wanted to shove the fearful thoughts right out of my mind, spring my wings open, and return to myself right then and there. But a wiser part of me saw this moment as a critical one, as my chance to use the full power of this contraction *to reverse itself.* So I put a fresh log on my metaphorical fire, opened my mind a half-degree more, and let my brain continue its agitated ride, fueled by the curiosity of what I would find.

My mind raced on and on. What about gas for the car? Gas for the stove? Where would I store the extra gas tanks? And electricity for the fridge? Would I need a generator? And heat for the house? The winters can get chilly, even in Sicily. Hmm.

My thoughts took a more practical day-to-day turn. Toilet paper. Toothpaste. Tampons. Q-tips. Paper for the computer. Ink for the printer. Pens for the desk. Books to read. Soap for the dishes. If soap is not around, perhaps paper plates would do. They are easy. Paper plates, cups, and forks . . . and serving dishes, too. Maybe the water from the Mediterranean could be used to wash the pots and pans. Yes, that would surely help.

It was precisely at this point that I started to giggle inside. With no effort at all, with no forcing, placing, or shoving of racing thoughts this way or that, with no striving to reopen myself after having been so completely and absurdly closed down, with no clinging to the image of the ideal me, the one who wouldn't be caught dead being anything other than steady and strong . . . the giggle rose up and out. It was the most natural thing in the world.

Although I'd been on an island at the time, one that had been invaded often through the centuries and had suffered unimaginable horrors, in that moment I realized that I wasn't an island. And no matter what horrors (imagined or otherwise) I might face in my life, I didn't want to ever try to be an island again. I couldn't live without others outside of a natural flow. And more importantly, even if I could, even if I figured out a way to organize a life like that, *I really, really, really didn't want to.* My heart opened wide and tossed away a huge chunk of fear. The caged bird stepped over the rubble, spread her wings, and powered by a fresh breath, flew high, high, high.

A mere four or five minutes were all that it took for me to lighten that day. Four or five minutes of indulgence of a fearful heart and over-active brain, letting my fear power my contraction, and this very contraction do the work that set me a little more free.

stepping aside

When you face an emotion directly, as I did with my anger that day, you absorb it and let it charge each cell of your skin. It's a warrior approach, a kind of I'm-bigger-than-anything-that-tries-to-shrink-or-dislodge-me attitude. As we saw with my example, using an emotion as a change-agent can be quite effective, but there's also another gentler and equally productive way to get out from under an emotion's embrace. Very simply, you can step aside from the emotion to find pure air to breathe. Then you can let the clarity of this new air refresh you, restore perspective, and point out your next step to take.

But can we really just step aside, you ask? Yes. It's actually quite easy. We do it nearly every day, in fact, when we feel the urge to pee then put it aside . . . until it becomes *urgent,* that is.

I think the experience of labor provides a wonderful parallel, too. When labor contractions begin, their pain is so great, that to absorb them would quickly bring even the strongest woman to her knees. Expectant mothers learn to separate themselves from the contractive force (or resort to pain killers instead!). Each contraction becomes a trigger to focus on something else—like positive visualizations or the movement of the breath. And the goal of these contractions, don't forget, is to soften and open the tissue so a new life can be born.

We can return to our feathered friends for another look at this. There are simply some winds that are too strong to ride. A better option is to go back to the nest. Or if the winds are manageable, but your feathers are still too ruffled for your tastes, you can find a willing branch to hang out on for a bit. It's a brief "slip into neutral gear," giving yourself a break. A connected disconnection, a slightly different relationship to the day. You see what's going on around you, but you're safely out of the wind.

If you've been used to managing, for example, to being in the front of the V formation leading the team, but are feeling stale or burned-out, a temporary "slip into neutral gear" might help. You can let someone else lead a meeting or suggest the next organizational change. It could be a nice stretch for the other person, as well as give you a fresh perspective. It's a natural, flexible movement.

I'm not asking you to pretend to feel anything that isn't true. That would go against everything I believe. We're just exploring the subtle differences between holding back, giving up, and finding a neutral gear.

Picture yourself at an office, party, or family reunion. Imagine you see some people you don't like come into the room. What would it feel like if you ignore your annoyance and are simply polite to them instead? Even if they say something that you normally react to, imagine that you stay calm—while in the middle of everything, enjoying your detached view.

Or if you are used to putting yourself in the middle of someone else's argument, solving other people's problems, or being the first one that people turn to for advice, feel yourself taking a time out from this role. This gives you a new role, and them the chance to climb out on their own.

Let me clarify something here, I'm not asking you to pretend to feel anything that isn't true. That would go against everything I believe. We're just exploring the subtle differences between holding back, giving up, and finding a neutral gear. So with no particular example in mind, find the neutral place inside yourself right now. Using your energy as a guide, slip into neutral gear. Now let's take it one step further. Find the open, connected, *and* neutral place within yourself. Where you can be calm, objective, *and* fully, vibrantly alive. Where you can have a clear mind, open heart, *and* fill every cell of your skin. Notice how your view of yourself and the world expands. Breathe in the possibility.

Feel your energy now. Has it lifted?

Slipping into neutral gives us the time to break old habits and untie ourselves from our knots. It's a holding pattern for flight, a chance to reflect, and an opportunity to reach in and find new parts of ourselves. New tones of voice that we want to use in this moment, today. Reactions that are actually *ours* and not just traditions from our past. In every moment, we have the power to choose who we really are and what we really, really want to do, say, or be. And this momentary stepping aside is often the very move we need to be willing to make to uncover a more authentic way.

flying high

stop, breathe, clear, expand, create

As a wave of creativity is sweeping you off your feet it's relatively easy to go along for the ride. You feel that energy bubbling up from within you, spilling over to the outside. But when you seem to have lost the wave, when no inspiration is to be found, what's to be done? Soleira Green claims that you can be in charge of your own energetic expansion and of everything that happens to you in your life. "Yup, everything," she adds, with a twinkle in her eye.

She teaches experts, the energetic elite, and uses a different language than we've been using, but not so different that we can't fit in. So I'm catching her pass and bringing that ball now to you. Follow with me in an example. Really try to feel into this thing.

You're going to do a speech for a small group: at the church, school, office, a Tupperware party, wherever. Yes, you are nervous. Most of us would be. You might think to yourself, "Will I do ok? Will I know what to say?" You might fear making a fool of yourself, even in the tiniest way. You might fret over what to wear or if your hair's just right. You might worry whether anyone will actually be there or not, or maybe that too many people will show up. As these thoughts race inside your head, your energy drops, your fields draw in. You get smaller and smaller, taking up less of the room that you're in.

But now you remember—*"Ah, I can be in charge of this!"*

STOP: Take that same nervousness and know that it's not you.

BREATHE: You breathe (breathe in, please) and exhale. Just for good measure, do it again.

CLEAR: Ask your mind to put all fears and concerns aside, to sweep away all whirling little thoughts. This takes no energy at all for you're not stuffing them back in . . . you're moving them to the side, gently letting them go for now.

EXPAND: Now, feel yourself expanding like a gigantic balloon, getting bigger and bigger. Your heart keeps you centered while your edges expand out further and further to give you lots of space to be you.

CREATE: From this expanded you, ask what wants to be said. Don't ask yourself what's in your head or on your notes, what the people might want you to say, or even what has been said on this subject before. Ask, instead, what wants to be said to bring both this speech and the people you'll be delivering it to, to the very best they can be. The twist in this plot is that you are not in control, the power of creation is. You are a partner to it, a surfer on its wave.

Allow the energy of what wants to be said to rise up from within. It may feel like a tingling all around you, a warmth in your heart, or a wave rising out of the ocean of your soul. Let that energy speak to you and through you without trying to control a single thing. Let your heart sing the song of the profoundness of its potential. As for the speech that results, the audience will hang on every word. And you will amaze even yourself at what you will say and who you will be. Try it and see.

Courtesy of Soleira Green, taken from the Leadergenics Internet e-course.

opening choices

When I was sick, I had to open to the possibility that a cure could exist to what the medical community was calling an incurable illness. Then I had to put my analytical engineer's brain aside to open to the touch of the complementary medicine healers that I used. I can remember feeling so vulnerable and raw, both embarrassed and intrigued by the path that I took. But through the power of that very vulnerability I was able to change my life.

Years later, when I'd decided to study Italian and retrace my family's roots, we literally reopened my granddad's Sicilian apartment that had been locked tight for the fifteen years since his death—a fitting metaphor, I thought. Again, I can remember the vulnerability that I felt as my life-long dream of being able to communicate with this part of my family was realized. And how I had to sidestep my training in polite conversation when the measly vocabulary that I'd learned couldn't keep up with my numerous thoughts. Luckily, I found that my open heart spoke well without words.

So the next time you're faced with a challenging task, opening even more fully to its possibility could be just the trick that changes the tide.

Let's take another example. I remember an important project of mine that was briefly stalled out. Dejected and confused, I wrestled with how I could get it moving again. Reaching under my anger, I put my frustration into more meaningful words, and felt to see if the possibility of greatness for this project still existed. With the project firmly in mind, I put my attention on my heart and was pleased to find a slight tingling sensation there. A few seconds later, I felt my heart lift and soar in a confirmation that it, indeed, wanted the project to continue. Then mustering up a healthy dose of courage and renewing my confidence that I had what it took to get the job done, I pried open my heart even further to make room for the possibility that my dream would come true, and soon. This wasn't a one-time visualization or morning meditation, by the way. I walked around *all day* with my heart expanded intentionally. It even hurt a bit because my heart had been so annoyed and rusted shut before. And within a few days, the momentum of the project began to rebuild by itself. Soon, I found myself swept up by *its* wave.

Take this moment to feel what's important to you right now. What hope is left within you, what dream would you like to dust off? What urge is stirring, what wants to come out? Perhaps it's an idea that you have. A question you'd like an answer to. A book you'd like to write. A change you'd like to see happen. A feeling you'd like to generate. An interest you'd like to explore. A relationship you want to nurture. Then with that thing in mind, open your heart to the possibility that one day soon this thing can and will exist.

Whether it's the next brushstroke on a canvas, the gentle stroke you'll place on someone's cheek, or the stroke of genius that will win you the Pulitzer Prize, whether it's a big, way-out-there dream or a very small thing that wants to happen through you right now . . . open your heart to it, give it the room to fly. Using your breath as a bellows, with your next three or four breaths, gently expand your heart's energy out. When you're the size that you like—plump, juicy, and ripe—picture yourself lifting off the ground in a hot air balloon like Dorothy's at the end of *The Wizard of Oz.* But instead of being nervous like she was, feel yourself confident and flexible with the movement. Wave to your friends down there on the ground. Feel their excitement for you. You are alive with potential and possibility.

Now tell me, as you feel your skin, is it tingling?

Souls are meant to move, to spur us on, to unfold like flowers in spring. It's up to you to discern whether your soul's stirring means to move out or up, to flee or fight, or to simply let things be. You get to choose. Fly on the wings of your soul, I say. And simply ignore the rest.

Eighty percent of people who completed these exercises reported a marked increased proficiency in flying. A solid twelve percent of participants found that they successfully bounced back from even gnarly domestic quarrels after brief ten-minute recovery periods—occasionally making their partners' heads spin. All groups reported that less chocolate was needed to satisfy an inner hunger. And although emotional swings from bad to good were still viewed as rare in the adult world, kids seemed to understand them just fine.

let the games begin: In this playground, we'll first work on tuning our awareness to the shrinking moments we have in our day, those magical, pivotal moments that hold the possibility of freshness. Then we'll play with reopening after we catch ourselves closing down. We'll end this step with getting beneath our contractions and expansions to find the urge of creativity trying to make its way up . . . and out. In Soar (Step 7), we'll ride this creative wave at full force. Finally, in Glow (Step 8), we'll create a superhighway from our most vital, passionate selves to the outer world.

Our first game in this step's playground is a physical one and perhaps the chapter's most important. It triggers our muscle memory and sets our stage. So if you're ready, roll up your sleeves (both figuratively and literally) and let the games begin.

1. movement is mandatory. Stand up and give yourself plenty of room. We're going to fly. First, let's contract. Curl yourself up into a standing ball. Put your head down, wings in, and tighten your stomach muscles as much as you can. Bend your knees if you'd like. Feel the force your contraction holds, the tension of a well-oiled spring. Then hold your breath, tensing up even further if you can. Just a few seconds of contraction is all that you need.

Now stand up, arms out, and take fresh air in. Put your head and shoulders back, chin toward the ceiling, wings wide to each side. You'll form a big T. Overachievers, from this position, pull your wings even further back, opening your chest wide. Contract the muscles between your shoulder blades to get into a fully-open stance.

Repeat the full range of motion, very slowly, six times. Breathe out on the contraction, breathe in for the soar.

2. out-of-the-box. Rate each of the following from one to ten. One is where you feel the most tension and limitation in your movements. Ten is where you feel the most creative, invigorated, and "open"—the sky's the limit, no constraints, boxes, or bounds. Remember, this is a feeling exercise, not a thinking thing. Overachievers, identify any area(s) where your logical brain says that you should be happy with what you've got, but your heart still doesn't feel fulfilled.

- Your work
- Your play
- Your love life
- Your family life
- Your extended family life
- Your world as a whole

3. your shrink, part one. Let's look at your "shrink"—not the psychological kind, the energetic one. Perhaps you're the dramatic type that crumbles or deflates in a sudden movement when a dream or hope is dashed, then rebounds the instant the winds align once again. Or perhaps you're the responsible type whose lift can be dampened by a general feeling of heaviness or burden—a movement so natural and gradual, so comfortable to your strong muscles, that at times you barely notice how you might labor under its weight. Or maybe you generally keep yourself pretty clear throughout the day, but have built up a slight residue of habit or apathy that dulls your natural shine.

Circle your favorite ways to shrink from the following list: crumble, collapse, complete shutdown, sulk, tiptoe around, crouch down, hunch over, cower, deflate, become invisible, dampen, dull, become cynical, criticize, run away, disappear, hold back, tense up, pity yourself, pout, scowl, lash out, give up, take a nose dive, start a fight. Overachievers, invent words of your own.

4. your shrink, part two. Notice each time that you shrink today. Overachievers, keep a list. And if you'd like, next to each one, jot down how long it took you to get back to full size, regardless of whether the initial problem was completely resolved or not. Did you bounce back in ten minutes, ten hours, or did it take a good night's sleep? Or are you still energetically shrunken, heavy, or dulled?

5. your shrink, part three. Over the next week, continue to notice each time that you shrink. See if you can spot the following movements:

- When you feel the "oldness" of your shrink and see a fresh way to respond—*immediately*. This could be as simple as changing a tone of voice you might normally have used.
- When you feel that a reopening isn't possible *at the moment* and you're temporarily stuck—not without

options, mind you, but objectively there's just no "wind" for fresh movement (at least not yet).

- When you feel, most certainly, that no forward movement will *ever* be possible with this other person, activity, or idea, that it's time to move on.

6. movement is mandatory, reprise. Stand up again and do another three or four full flaps of those mighty wings. But this time instead of pretending to be a wound-up powerful spring bursting forth, pretend to be a butterfly resting on a pink rose and let a warm wave of love rise up to open you. Delicate. Gracious. Sunlit. Real.

7. your split-second decision: open or close. During her last year of high school, Georgia, a beautiful, intelligent athlete, lost all of her shoulder-length blonde hair to an auto-immune disease called alopecia areata. As the path of this illness became clear, Georgia felt a split-second choice present itself: to close up tight or open herself even more fully to the world. She chose to open.

When a mother of three lost her husband to a sudden heart attack, she could have closed down and used tranquillizers to take away the pain, but she didn't. *"Sally, this is one I have to feel,"* is what she said to me that day.

When I was learning Italian, after two weeks of total immersion, I reached the point where my brain was full, my head ached, I'd had it. But instead of closing down, I chose to open my mind to let it find a new pathway to use. It hurt a little at first, then the tension eased, and new words found their way to me.

Have you ever had a split-second choice moment when you decided to open further rather than close down?

8. high impact open-close. Think back to September 11, 2001. Initially, did you open more or close more as a result of that day? And now?

9. so your back's to the wall. Feeling suffocated? Trapped? Lost? Scared? A little rigidity isn't always a bad thing. Hitting up against it actually has the power to open us up wider than we've been before, both literally and figuratively.

To prove this, find a physical rigidity somewhere in the room—any doorjamb will do. Then as a cat might, press the fleshy part on one side of your spine up against the hardness of the wall. Let the rigid wall massage you. Move to the fleshy part on the other side of your spine and repeat the exercise. Breathe as you expand into the contraction.

10. clear the air. Think back to the last argument you had (or one that is brewing). Then reach below the surface tension to what really, really wants to be said. Ask yourself the simple question, *What's really going on here?* Then reach in and see what gems you pull out.

11. anger as a fuel. Anger can be a potent fuel for change. A daughter's murder drives a parent to speak out. A layoff forces a rethinking of an entire career. A botched trial spurs legal reform. Tempers flare. Political movements get started. Foundations and charities get formed. Identify with the most precision you can what you are most angry about, if anything.

12. love as a fuel. One simple infatuation can cause a person to take flight, abandoning old habits and taking untold risks. True love can build a foundation for amazing growth. When one is loved, it's much easier to spread one's wings. Poems get written.

Children conceived. New ideas born. Has love ever spurred you to do something that you never thought you'd do before?

13. mindless bounce-back. Bouncing back doesn't have to be rational, to make sense to our minds. It can be as simple as a directed movement of energy. Let's try it, and see.

- **GET BIG, PHYSICALLY.** As you read these words, bring your attention to your physical body position. Notice spots of tension. Adjust yourself to get more comfortable, starting with opening your breath up wide. Head up. Relax your shoulders. Loosen your jaw. Shift in your seat. Do whatever you need to do to feel as big as you can in the position you're in right now.

- **GET BIG, WITH NO EFFORT AT ALL.** As you read these words, think about something stressful. Feel the contraction begin, your energy sinking, your muscles aching. Now, using absolutely no effort at all, with a simple expansion of your invisible wings, reverse the energetic smallness without changing a thing about the situation itself. Feel the tension lifting, peeling itself away from your physical form. With each of your next few breaths, wash another layer of stress from your body. Again. And again. And again. You are clean, clear, whole. Let your energy expand even further, no matter what tension is around. You're the size of your skin. Now you are as big as the room. The house. The neighborhood. Keep breathing. Within you is the entire world.

- **GET BIG, EVEN FASTER.** Imagine you hit a huge traffic jam as you headed to work and are late for a meeting. Or your fly is open as you get introduced to the President. The dinner burns minutes before guests arrive. You lose your job. You gain ten pounds. Pick your favorite idea of hell on earth and with one in-breath and out-breath, bring your energy back to its heavenly state.

- **GET BIG, EVEN WHEN THE ANSWER IS UNKNOWN.** Sometimes it's years before we understand the purpose of turbulent times. Let's play with bringing more comfort to them in the meanwhile. Think of one thing that's in the works that you don't have a complete answer for, it's either a full or partial "unknown." Now, with a few good breaths, clear your air, and let go of some of the tension that you feel. With another breath, expand into the silence of this very moment, into the power of the unknown. Now with a final breath, breathe in the profound possibility of what is yet to come.

14. movement is mandatory, a spin unspun. Remember the exercise from Walk (Step 4) called "Go for a Spin?" Let's do it again and see how far we've come. Put your arms out to the side in your favorite soar position. Then spin three times at your level of comfort in either direction. As professional dancers know well, dizziness will come . . . *and go.* For a dancer, a count of three is usually all it takes. How many seconds does it take you to get back to yourself after being thrown off-balance in this way?

15. do a flip. A "flip" is a movement from negativity to positivity, from a cup half-empty to one half-full. We've done it lots in this book already. We "flipped" when we looked at my old illness as a teacher rather than an enemy. We flipped the idea of how hard it is to shine, then tickled its belly and dis-covered that around certain people, shining is the most natural thing on earth to do. A

Seattle-area children's charity flipped the way it interviewed new kids wanting its services. It used to take kids' histories by probing their problems, failures, deficits, and shortcomings. Then it started asking positive questions during orientation, like what the kids wanted to get out of life and who was available to help them.

Let's flip right now. What gift did your last failure or difficulty bring you? Perhaps a closed-hearted boyfriend actually burst your heart wide open, something no one had ever done before. Or poverty taught you common sense. Or an extra-tight deadline brought out the best in you.

16. sugar and spice, and everything nice. Were you raised to be every parent's dream, oh-so-nice-and-polite? To be seen and not heard? To hold your opinions to yourself? For this exercise I want you to open to the possibility that this is a habit you can now give up.

As general manager, I knew enough to harness the power of all the team members rather than stick with just the handful of people at the top of the pyramid. Each person's input was valuable. Sure, it meant that we had to keep ourselves open, to ask lots of questions, and to make people comfortable approaching the management team with any idea they had. It was often a well-stated complaint that showed us exactly what we needed to do to accelerate our forward movement.

For this exercise, sometime today, offer your opinion on something to someone to whom you've never offered an opinion before. Overachievers, ask someone else for an opinion, someone whom you've never asked before. Then open to the possibility that something terrific will result.

17. the right support. There are times when we need to be nurtured, when our wings feel shaky and weak. But when we've recovered, with wings strong and wide, look out! A close hug could feel suffocating. A nurturing voice could be an irritation. Depending on which side of the support/supporter relationship you are on today, notice if this dynamic is at play.

18. demand more of them. Who are you helping stay the least bit "smaller" by not demanding the "more" that you know they have inside?

19. movement is mandatory, move it up. Soul movement is not a thinking thing—rational, calculated, and planned. It's a nonsensical feeling, often simultaneously surprising, delighting, and frustrating us with its twists, turns, and bends. Feel underneath any emotions you may be feeling right now and see if you can identify an urge that wants to come up . . . and out. It might be a simple idea, a change you'd like to see happen, an interest you'd like to explore, a relationship you want to nurture, or something you'd like to create. If you can't, that's okay, too. Maybe it's your time to rest.

20. movement is mandatory, move it out. Keep your energy moving by walking, dancing, stretching, or some other form of exercise today.

wrap-up

This step asks us to stop playing even the least bit small and open our wings out wide to the world. It asks our hearts to remember, without any doubt, that humans have always been meant to fly. Then without even having to be asked, our souls, who are always listening, feel themselves starting to stir. With space to breathe and room to move, they give us the wind for our wings.

step 7, soar

GOAL: GIVE UP THE EFFORT AND SOAR WITH THE WIND. *In this step we stretch our energetic muscles into the "fully-open" position . . . then open wider, wider, and wider yet, breaking free to embrace our inner wave of passion. As this force lifts us up from within, we open to the possibility of the magic that it carries. Pleasurable breezes greet us, adding their support for each inspiration.*

beyond belief

"I'd lose myself in my crank-mode, as I called it, and *soar*," I once told a therapist, happily remembering periods of unlimited vitality. I loved to soar, to accomplish more in a day than I'd normally do in a week. I'd felt such peace. Such power. Such safety, though I wasn't sure why traveling at such high speeds felt safer to me, but it did. It was a more natural pace, one I would have used more often if I weren't so worried about fitting in. They were breaks from normal human limits, opportunities to burst out, stretch my wings, fly free.

"Ever since I was a little girl, I'd had flying dreams," I continued. They'd begun with my leaping off tall buildings and gliding safely to the ground. Then they built to where I could take off from a lawn and reach the roof of a building.

As I got more experienced, I'd bypass the roofs altogether, past the tops of the trees, effortlessly climbing over entire towns—worlds, even—and back again. The wide-open span of my arms and chest was my only force. I could do whatever I wanted, whenever I wanted, with this openness. The winds were both outside me and within me, happy friends at playtime.

As delighted as I was recounting my tale, the therapist was equally concerned. "Escaping" and "losing myself" like this were perhaps a bit less than productive, he said. Finding my footing on the ground, in the real world, might be a better choice to make. My bubble burst. I started to cry.

Now I can see that the therapist was wrong. There is nothing bad about soaring, defying limitations, breaking free of barriers, and flying through the mundane. At minimum, it gives you a good perspective.

And at best, it provides an effortless ride to heights that you've

Humans are a lovely mixture of the profound and the mundane. Our ability to soar tips the scales a bit, allowing us both to reach higher heights . . . and glide through the routine.

only dreamed you could attain, turning the winds of change into allies, and enticing the winds of passion to lift you up from the inside out, spreading your wings, powering your flight.

I usually soar about a week to ten days at a time, a dozen or so times a year, occasionally more. These are the weeks where fifty or one hundred pages get written, parties get planned, contacts get made, contracts signed, new seasons begin, new ideas born . . . and more than one friend holds their head in bewilderment at the change from just one week before.

The key ingredients, you ask? The courage to leave the nest, leap off that branch, or make a bold directional change. Muscles strong enough to get you to the right currents, limber enough to change velocities at will, and a wing span sure enough to invite your deepest passions to rise. Then, opening wider than you've ever opened before, you catch the next breeze, the invisible force that's waiting to carry you with ease to new heights.

Or, to put it more bluntly, you have to get your butt off whatever branch you may be hanging out on, whatever cliff edge you're clinging to, and get into that wind, knowing you have the capability to handle even a hurricane if need be. *Then stop working so damned hard,* yakking with those mouths, flapping those wings. Yep, it's this last part that's relatively easy for all-talk-no-action types, but is a killer for the doer-bees in the crowd, those people used to taking responsibility for everyone and everything, climbing higher only through the hardest of work, the tightest of schedules, and the most detailed plans.

The winds are here to partner with us, to drive and support us—inside and out. They rise up from within, taking the form of our passions, providing the fuel to power our moves. They play with us from afar, teasing us with possibilities, and dancing up to us in the form of a synchronistic whim. We catch wind of something new and feel the support of coincidences that come our way. Inside and out, the winds are here to serve us. Opening to them is the goal of this step.

Humans are a lovely mixture of the profound and the mundane. Our ability to soar tips the scales a bit, allowing us both to reach higher heights . . . and glide through the routine. Every experience we have in life helps us to live it: the pleasant surprises, loving touches, acts of kindness, achievements, natural wonders, vacations, as well as those experiences that are nasty, disappointing, or sad. Actors can't pretend to feel something they've never experienced. Writers can't put words to a powerful sensation they can't imagine having. Painters can't bring an emotion to the canvas that they don't have the capacity to hold themselves. And humans can't soar without the ability to open up and experience all that life has to offer. Any resistance to either the "good" or the "bad" keeps one foot on the ground. A sincere and humble openness is key.

Timing is another important factor in soaring. You can't force your passion to come out, just as you can't force a gentle breeze to come your way. But as my Italian cousins say, once the wave of inspiration comes, you have no choice but to ride it. It's one of the few valid reasons to leave home or skip a Sunday dinner.

An executive once told me that his wings had been clipped since a recent merger as he'd waited for the reorganization to settle out. "I am so tired of them concentrating on selling buildings and other small business units to boost short-term profits. We sit in these all-day meetings that are so dull, deciding what we can trim or sell next . . . I want them to give me an impossible goal and set me loose *to make it happen!*" He was going stir-crazy, inner juices flowing, craving a solid several-month soar.

My cousin Tina in Sicily has a method of daily soaring, though I'm sure she wouldn't use that word to describe it. To her, soaring seems too natural to be anything other than ordinary, though no one I've introduced her to would agree.

Tina cooks dinner for twelve without mussing a hair, weaving the freshest ingredients the market has to offer together with the tastes of the guests into a thoroughly satisfying feast. Three kinds of *cannoli,* homemade ice cream, two vegetable side-dishes, five types of fish. Two more people coming? No problem. Just pull up the chairs. Anyone else would be brought to his or her knees. But then again, "anyone else" may not love cooking the way she does, put such passion into it, and feel such a strong wave of inspiration from bringing the family together around the dinner table.

There was one day, in particular, that I'll never forget—the day Mom and I coined the expression, *"to pull a Tina."* After the soup course, Tina whipped out an elaborate casserole in a ceramic dish that would fit a decent-sized turkey. Each piece of pasta—barely bigger than a large grain of rice—had been hand-rolled by Tina, then mixed in with cheese, sauce, spices, and the meat that she'd freshly ground. It was a complicated dish, fit to serve a king.

"When in the world did she have time to do this?" Mom and I asked ourselves. We were together the entire night before and that whole morning. A glance into the kitchen revealed a few stray things on the counter, but no clear evidence of any sizeable activity. "Was it frozen?" we asked. Surely it had to have been prepared in advance. "This? It's nothing, really," Tina said. "I did it as I watched TV after you two went to bed last night."

An hour and a half of relaxing time for her, where for us it would have been a huge project, dirtying every pot and pan we'd had, taking days to plan, hours to execute, and a fanfare afterwards to celebrate its completion. The look on Tina's face made us realize that we, ourselves, were creating our own confusion—fighting the wind, so to speak. Life, indeed, could be less burdensome and depleting if we were open to it being so. Floors could be swept to the beat of our favorite songs. Projects could move along with hitches being handled. Money could be made doing things we love to do. And maybe, just maybe, our upcoming flight back to the States didn't need to exhaust us at its thought, fill us with the dread of rushed schedules, heavy traffic, and even heavier bags.

We decided to try an experiment—*"to pull a Tina"* during our trip home. Five enormous suitcases stuffed with Italian delicacies, a two-hour taxi ride through the narrow Sicilian streets, the chaotic Catania airport, the wait in the smoky lounge, the hour-long flight to Rome, the negotiation with the clerk over our overweight bags, and the separate transatlantic flights to our respective homes—all went as smooth as glass, as simple as pie. We arrived fresh and relaxed, soared right through it, so to speak, then giggled to each other at how simple a difficult thing could be. Once again, openness and engagement being the key.

open wide

Imagine waking up each day fully "open" to the world around you—arms out, chest wide, heart exposed, guard down. Imagine further that nothing happens to "close" you, no punch, no shrinking, no doubts. Work deadlines, rush hour traffic, jam-packed shopping malls, stinky buses, even stinkier diapers, long airport lines, crying kids, rude people, criticisms, disappointments, disagreements, complaints, rejections, news reports, burned dinners, household bills, daily duties, lids up on toilet seats . . . none of these phase you one little bit. You're beyond using your energetic muscles on the mundane. Your perspective is simply bigger than that. Your view is huge, even with your feet on the ground.

What piques your interest are the new sights that catch your eye, draw your attention, stir your juices, and come to your aid. You feel secure, calm, open, vital, empowered, passionately connected to the world, in partnership with the wind. You've learned that the trick to soaring is to be both relaxed and engaged. You've felt that sweet spot.

Your only discomfort comes when the wind's power moves through you at a pace faster than you've ever felt before, vibrating each cell of your body, sending shivers down your spine, putting a tremor in your hand. "Can I go to an even higher height, do I deserve this, can I handle it?" you ask yourself, knowing full well that you don't want to say no to those questions anymore. You can feel stretched and anxious, but driven to continue. Giddy on the outside and calm at the core. That familiar push-pull of the soul.

Then with a decisive in-breath and out-breath, you open your mind and let the big, bigger, biggest thought in. You agree to follow those inner urges and do what that deepest part of you wants you to. You accept that new role, have that child, adopt that pet, move to that new city, go on that trip, take or teach that class, read or write that book, experiment with that hairstyle, paint that room, learn that language, make that friend, sell that thing, move into that house, join that church, get that new furniture, go to that health spa, attend that lecture, form that group, help that charity . . . or in whatever form it takes, take that step that vibrates the winds inside of you.

You smile at others who think of "open" as naïve, easy-to-manipulate, or the height of vulnerability. You know it's the safest and most powerful place to be.

Your energetic muscles, trained and vibrant, hold you open and wide. You climb higher and higher on a flight that is made both by you and for you, with the support of someone who "gets" you a mere shout, phone call, e-mail, or handshake away. Your perspective is immeasurable. Strength takes a soft, receptive form. Surprises cease to surprise you. There's no difference between "good" and "bad." Synchronicities line the path, brought in by the wind. And although an occasional wave of nausea can come along, you know it's entirely curable with but a few deep breaths and a little settling time. You smile at others who think of "open" as naïve, easy to manipulate, or the height of vulnerability. You know it's the safest and most powerful place to be.

Remember those B-movies where the heroine (why is it always a woman, I ask?), wearing a flowing-white-something, is being chased by the bad guy? She inevitably falls down, crying and anxious, giving the villain just enough time to catch her. Why? Because she has a mind that's scared, needy, and *closed.* Her sharpness is gone, flexibility zip. Any creativity she may have possessed is out the window.

Now we're not talking about the Olympics here, no super-human feats would be required to get that damsel in distress to safety. Just the presence of mind to have not opened the damned door for that guy in the first place (she could have *felt* he was a creep, even if she couldn't hear the movie's background music), screamed for help (those vocal chords *can* still work, you know), used the telephone (they aren't *always* ripped out), locked the door (in Italy they even have bullet-proof ones), hidden in a great spot (ask any kid where), made the pepper in the kitchen into a spray (Martha Stewart can show us how), found that golf club and used it (hear us roar!), or ran in a direction other than the steepest and deepest part of the woods (duh!), or jumped over (instead of stumbled over) the branch that's fallen across the path (it's rarely *that* high).

And I don't know about you, but I'm ready to see a small-shouldered, ultra-feminine, lipstick-lined gal hike up her flowing white skirt, fly through that foggy night, leap over those dimly-lit trees, spot the shortcut, and soar to the light of day on the other side, breaking only a nail or two of her well-manicured fingertips. Bad guys outwitted, a nice healthy glow attained, minus the cost of a personal training session, to boot. Yes, that sounds about right, and about time. The power of a spry, alert, and agile openness.

This fantasy finally out there, let's return once again to the land of the genuinely imperfect human being named Sally.

When I was given a one-way ticket to a new life and almost lost it fighting to protect the old.

leaving the nest

It was spring. Alone in my office, as I closed the cabinet doors and turned toward my desk, a strong sensation filled me, a sense of closure, a job finished. There was no sadness with it, no emptiness either. It was a simple period at the end of a sentence, a stamp marked "complete."

Sure there were things on my to-do list, projects that needed attention. But if I'd learned anything by that point, it was that there were two distinct worlds going on at the same time, the one visible to our eye and another playfully hiding under our skin. The latter spoke through emotions, inner drives, and openings. It brought sudden urges, new perspectives, and fire for our passions. This voice boomed, *"Your job here is complete. It's time to move on."*

And you'd think I would have also learned by then that an urge of this urgency was always, always right . . . and in the end would win out over logic. But with the imperfection of this Sally, I chose to ignore it, preferring the comfort of my vice president position instead. My inner world grumbled, muscles bulging through the bars of its freshly padlocked cage.

Our next quarter was a roaring success. The team was flying high. In a dream, my soul broke free, and I became an eagle in flight. I flew not alone, but with other eagles, occasionally soaring past each other, then disappearing as we completed our individual circles before meeting up once again. A moment later, I was a little girl licking her favorite ice cream cone.

Back at the office, my dream came true. For the first time in our history, every corporate division bested its predictions.

Our stock doubled, then tripled. Our future looked bright. But a month after that, I learned that my division was to be sold—"merged," actually, with a multi-billion-dollar international conglomerate. I was spinning in a push-pull vortex, my brain holding on to its job title while my soul and outer world were breaking free. My world was like a volcano, turning itself inside out.

Get to the mountains, now, my inner voice commanded. And this time I didn't ignore it. A friend and I hiked to Mt. Rainier's Camp Muir. Situated on a permanent snowfield with glaciers above and on each side, it's my eagle's nest, my room with a view, my place to reflect. We awoke to a foot of fresh snow and climbed down in white-out conditions. This is how it's going to be for a while, I thought, noting the irony of the symbolism.

"Six months," I'd told the president when he'd broken the news. *"I'll stay six months for the transition. That's it!"*

I'd expected that the words had come out in anger, meant to make my boss feel guilty, mad, or both. That they weren't the slightest bit true and would feel inconsistent, slimy, and unclean. Instead, I felt a sweet resonance with my words, a connection to a truer world within. But still, at the company I stayed, dedicated executive that I was, my soul twiddling its thumbs.

Even before the merger was final, people started asking for raises, reaching for money as a substitute for the heartfelt satisfaction that we'd felt before. Our energy flattened. Resignations became commonplace.

A pressure to protect the team built inside of me until I thought I would explode. I didn't relapse, thankfully, but a different kind of breakdown occurred. One day I left the car door wide open in my driveway for over a half hour—purse, phone, and groceries in plain sight. The next day, I left my car running in the parking lot after returning from lunch. Then about a week later, I drove away from a gas station with the hose still inserted into the car's tank. I literally ripped the thing right off, dragging it halfway across the parking lot before I realized what I'd done.

As soon as I could, I went on vacation in Arizona. I couldn't quite bring myself to fully relax, but at least I could finally breathe. One evening, alone in a mountain cabin I'd rented, I began the very first draft of this book.

The merger closed a short time later, the official paperwork finally in place. Controls were coming down all around us. Figures that had been looked at monthly were asked for on a weekly, even daily, basis. The words "team member" were replaced by "employee" in our new human resources handbook. More and more decisions were being made behind closed doors by the privileged few, the results handed down in formal memoranda. I hadn't been on the production floor for weeks. I felt disconnected from everything I knew as true.

Jamal, a friend and minister, met me for a short walk in the park. He listened intently, then volunteered with a huge smile, "I'll pray that whatever happens is for the highest good of all involved."

I'd have preferred a little sympathy, a solid complaint or two, a nasty jab at the faceless corporate giant who was taking away my precious company. But the prayer left me speechless in its grace, removing the lock on my soul's cage—for that night, at least. My inner voice waited patiently for me to recognize that the winds of change that were blowing were, once again, not an enemy, but a friend. Fear is but a trick of an over-active mind.

"They want machines, not people . . . and *I'm* supposed to support it!" I told Jessica one night. My voice showed its stress as I took another sip of holiday champagne, pretending that I wanted it. All I wanted was to find an end to the push-pull of my soul.

"Why don't you just leave?" Jessica responded. A fair question by any measure.

"Mostly to protect the team." I'd been fighting the new management's layoff plans for weeks, stalling until a new piece of business could be finalized and tensions eased.

"You're under a lot of pressure, Sally. Take care of yourself . . . You don't want to get chronically fatigued again!" Jessica said, adding a look that penetrated my skin.

She was right.

The merger had been my birth canal, with pressure on all sides. It had been a test of my connection with my feeling nature, and my willingness to align my inner and outer worlds. I'd passed, but barely, then celebrated New Year's in Arizona.

I flew home on January 7. My eyes were bright and clear. One week later, at 7:30 A.M. sharp, I walked into my new boss's office to entertain his offer of a position in a reorganization he was announcing, a polite formality that we both knew I would not accept.

Not surprisingly, before long I took a third trip to Arizona. As the Italians would say, *"Non c'è due senza tre,"* everything comes in threes. I entered the energy chiropractor's office a few minutes early. He worked in a group setting, ten tables at a time.

"If it feels comfortable, repeat after me," he whispered, his brown eyes sincere, compassionate and alert. *"It's not a matter of life or death anymore."* I repeated the phrase, long past wondering how these people knew what they knew.

"It's a matter of life or greater life," he added, then touched his fingers to my forehead, implanting the thought. I could feel my wings lift up then spread themselves wide.

A month or so later, as I listened to Mary Manin Morrissey's speech in a several-thousand person church hall, it felt like she was talking directly to me. She was describing how a mother eagle builds a nest. How thorns in the branches are critical in holding a nest tightly together. How the mother lines a nest with down and soft leaves.

"As the eaglets get older and it's time for them to begin to move on," the minister continued, "the mother eagle starts pulling away the down, pulling away the leaves . . . until there's this big thorny place that's prickly and pokey. As the eaglets begin to become dissatisfied with that, if they don't leave on their own, *she tosses them out.*" The crowd laughed at the image.

"Then as the eaglets begin to drop," she said, her tone turning deliberate, "they have a choice. They either crash or they spread their wings. If they will trust enough to spread their wings, they find that there are currents that absolutely delight to lift them."

Opening wide literally creates new possibilities. Options exist that never occurred to us before.

I, like these eagles, had been faced with a choice. Although I'd not been graceful by any definition of the term, I eventually came to my senses. I joined forces with the urge that had been rising up within me, opened to the invisible forces that surrounded me, then discovered that each supported my forward movement in the most natural, dependable way.

I soared for five years once I'd broken free. I traveled the world six months out of each year, starting relatively close to home, then catching stronger and stronger currents that took me farther and farther away. They brought me from the bottom of the Grand Canyon to the top of Africa's highest mountain, from the Sicilian shores of the Mediterranean to the ghettos that line that same sea along the Gaza Strip, from the inside of the King's Chamber in the Great Pyramid to sunrise on the top of Mount Sinai. With each circle I made of the globe, my view expanded, my passion's fire roared. Expand, open, expand, open wider, expand, open wider yet, soar . . . *glow!*

Then one day it all changed. My feet yearned to be back on the ground. My fingers longed to run through the hair I'd cut short. Both the tips of those fingers and my body itself yearned to create something inside. So with a swift downward move of my wings from open to closed, I cut through the air, and was propelled back home.

What is "focus" other than a swift downward movement of wings? What is "concentration" other than a positive form of a contraction? We lose perspective in a good way when we deliberately direct our attention into one area. All of these are simply choices of how we focus our energy. "Closed" doesn't necessarily mean "closed down."

Opening wide literally creates new possibilities. Options exist that never occurred to us before. People are aware without an angst underneath it, hopeful without one particular hope filling their minds. They are receptive, spontaneous, and responsive. Flexible, creative, and resourceful. People are most approachable when they are fully open. They have a patience and warmth. They bring a unique perspective to a discussion. An open person can see all sides of an argument and be a wise mentor and friend.

The beautiful thing about life is how many choices we have in it. When I returned home, it didn't mean that my soaring days were over—to the contrary. It was just a different kind of soar, one done with my feet on the ground, similar to the soar that I'd experienced during the years that I'd spent happily at the factory before my inner voice had changed its mind. One's passion can fill one's wings in any chosen style.

soaring through the routine

milking with maurice

Maurice was a dairy farmer in the small upstate New York town where I grew up, who shared with his son the twice-a-day milking duty of the cows. Twice a day, every day, 365 days a year, rain, snow, or shine. Maurice had a face so weathered that it almost appeared smooth. After his farming duties, he'd chat with my mom and dad, always picking the same captain's chair at our kitchen table, and always tipping back so the chair went on its hind legs as he stretched out his own. My mom would growl, fearing the chair would grow rickety and eventually fall apart altogether. But Maurice never changed, and the chair always held whomever wanted to sit in it—perhaps a little better than the others. It gave you a loose, floating feeling much like the sensation of soaring we are talking about here. A tinge out of control while perfectly safe at the same time.

Maurice liked to loosen up both things and people. A favorite target of his was the "city folk" from New York who'd come upstate on the weekends. He'd tell them how smart cows were, when truth be told, cows are quite the opposite. If cows go into a stall other than their own, they get so upset that their milk stops flowing. So day after day, to their exact same stall they return, with an occasional pause to view a neighbor's stall along the way. It was precisely at one of these pauses that Maurice would pipe up and say, "Bessy Sue, come a little farther down. Use this stall here, the third one on the right." Bessy Sue would "obey," as would the rest of the cows he commanded. The city folk stared on in amazement.

Maurice would then burst into a big belly laugh, the crinkles around his eyes flowing naturally into those covering the rest of his well-lined face. He was a man in the richest sense of the word. He knew that ice cream was best eaten after it had softened a bit, that politics failed the moment it forgot about the people it served, and that to stroke a rock that had gone through his tumbler would calm anyone right down. And when his thirty-eight-year-old son's girlfriend found out she was pregnant, he said, "Congratulations. It's about time."

Openness. Perspective. Sense of humor. These are the tools Maurice used to soar—feet firmly on the ground, hands in the soil, and heart opened wide.

Views take on a new importance, as does breaking free from the pack. Although cats are known to eat birds, they paradoxically become a kindred spirit to the majority of the people proficient in soaring because of a cat's tendency to prefer being alone rather than with someone it doesn't like. The heightened sense of comfort in one's own skin was correlated to an increase in the number of outbursts, breakthroughs, moments of standing up for oneself, or (if the cat is the guide) moments when one just walks away, uninterested and undisturbed. A minority of participants (the author included) reported an initial anxiety at the thought of giving up the fight. The idea of letting the wind carry them even a few feet was reported to cause nightmares, racing thoughts, and sweaty palms. Fortunately, after the experience of one solid soar, these symptoms immediately subsided.

It's your choice today, too. Do you want to remain open or closed, to fly or to soar, to rest on a branch or to break free? Knowing that with trained wings and a heartfelt connection every option is yours.

let the games begin: Soaring requires a partnership with pleasure, an allowing of ease, and a firm connection with oneself—not to mention giving up any tendency to take control, to grab the tiller, to battle the tide. Like so many things, soaring is a split-second choice we make. A simple one, but not always easy. And once made, it makes you wonder why it took you so long to say yes to it. Let the games begin.

1. movement is mandatory

- **PHYSICALLY.** Get into a fully-open soar position. Stand. Place your feet as wide apart as is comfortable. Head up, shoulders back, chest wide. Put your arms out to your side, and pull them back as far as they will go, using the muscles of your back to help you. Feel the stretch across your breast bone. Take three breaths and imagine yourself opening to the wind's full flow.

- **IN CONSCIOUSNESS.** Expanding your consciousness means stretching your awareness beyond its normal bounds. It's not a physical act, it's an energetic one. Stand. Position your feet comfortably under your hips. Place your hands loosely by your side, allowing them to move, but only when they want to. Breathe in and out three times to clear the air within and around you. Feel yourself in your skin. With your next breath, expand your energy outwards until it is a few inches larger than your physical form. Continue breathing into your energy until you feel it the size of the room. The neighborhood. The city. The world. Overachievers, try walking around the room staying this "big."

2. partnering with pleasure. Soaring with the wind is a marvelous sensation. To prepare ourselves for its pleasure, take the next five minutes and write a whole page list of the people, activities, and things that open you up wide, free your spirits, and make you warm inside. Then pick one at random and ask yourself why. Choose a few words to describe it. Finally, let two more people or things jump off the page to be enjoyed this very week. Jot them in your calendar or post them on the fridge as a reminder.

fill the page if you can!

fill that page!

3. cup completely full. Let's imagine that we've moved beyond Fly (Step 6) where we "flipped" our half-empty cups to view them as half-full, and now have cups that overflow every minute of every day with people, activities, and things that we really, really love—and laughter along the way.

As a symbol of this, Italian-style, eat exactly what you want for a week. Indulge those taste buds with your favorite tastes, satiate those inner appetites. Green eggs and ham for breakfast, sautéed mushrooms for lunch, a lovely piece of swordfish for dinner. You choose. And don't share even a morsel with another soul—unless you really, really want to, of course! Overachievers, if sharing is your thing, throw a dinner party; fix a feast of your fondest treats!

4. oh no, i'm different! When one is considering breaking away from the flock and going on a lovely soar, a wave of oh-no-I-don't-want-to-be-different-and-not-fit-in can come along. Let's play with this like we played with pain and anger before, stretching it to its limits, poking at its core.

Once upon a time there was a junior adman who was sent to present the original Marlboro Man idea to the gruff client who was known to chew up admen for breakfast. He'd huff and he'd puff and he'd discard all ideas. Then, as the junior adman presented a cowboy with the phrase "Come to where the flavor is," written below, the crotchety client nearly threw him out of the room. *"What flavor?"* he bellowed. *"You have to tell the public what to expect."* But the junior adman knew that the power of the ad was precisely because the flavor was to each and every person exactly what he or she wanted that flavor to be.

What "flavor" would you like to come home to? How is it different from your best friend's? Can you see that we are all a little bit different, that your "wings" may be short and quick-paced, and someone else's long and floppy? Can you appreciate that all wing shapes are useful in their own way?

5. break out. To practice breaking away from the pack, do at least one of the following, preferably in the next two minutes:

- Shout *"I believe!"* five times from your balcony or out your front door. Make that Baptist minister proud. Or try *"Good morning, world!"* in the style of Robin Williams' *"Good morning, Vietnam!"*
- Pick a theme song for yourself and let it rip, *Ally McBeal*-style. If you have no idea which one to choose, your favorite TV theme song will do just fine.

- Complete the following sentence, then shout it five times out loud. "I deserve _____." Don't write it down first. Let it come off the top of your head.
- Think about a break-out-of-the-box movie, like *Top Gun, Jerry Maguire,* or *Field of Dreams.* Overachievers, go rent it tonight.
- Crank up the stereo to your favorite station and dance around the room.
- Read the comics or your favorite childhood book. Overachievers, go see a live comedy show . . . or eat your favorite kid's cereal for every meal until the box is gone.

6. break free. During times of critical change, when we want to break free of a role we've played, a tradition we've honored, an attitude that's holding us back, a secret we've kept inside, an abuse that's beaten us up, a lack of confidence that's beaten us down, we often find the feeling of being "sick and tired" rev itself up as an inner fuel. Some of us physically get sick. Some of us just get tired. Overachievers like me do both.

When Jeanette wanted to break free in her mid-twenties, she moved to New York, 2,500 miles from her Oregon home. But she found that her real break came fifteen years later when she moved back to the northwest. "The physical break did just a small part of the job," she said. "It was after a trip to Egypt when I'd had two precious weeks to leave the world as I knew it and reconnect with myself, that my real progress began. I saw who I was, separate from my family—separate from everyone, in fact. And I knew that once I tasted this new me, I couldn't let her go. My conversations became more real. I didn't play the usual "good daughter" anymore. Now I can be me, let them be them, and not get as tweaked if they get anxious over a choice I've made. It's much better for everyone—*and so much less work!*"

With our sense of humor firmly intact and energetic muscles well-trained and limber, let's look at what we are sick and tired of right now (if anything). Let those aggravation bubbles rise. They're nothing to be afraid of, just bursts of energy that can be used to make a change, new choice, breakout, or breakthrough. Using your breath, allow any sick and tired sensation to rise up, responsibly, without acting out on it in any way. Imagine that instead of inside you, it is out in front of you. Take a good look at it, circling it a few times, studying its size, flexibility, and movements. Recognize it as an energy, a force, a vitality. If it's a gale-force, it's likely a breakthrough that it's offering, a generous supplement to your normal energy. Overachievers, ask it what it wants to say. Put fresh words to it. Then decide what you want to do next.

7. inner urge. If you've ever felt an undeniably clear inner urge, an intuitive voice from deep inside, did you do as I've done so many times and shove it back down, trying to return to well-known (even though not always entirely pleasant) solid ground? Or did you immediately give its suggestion a try?

8. confidence. Confidence doesn't have to be earned, it exists naturally. Look at any kid. At age six, my niece Paige commented, with a shake of her little head, "Adults like to do things the same way. Kids like to do everything their own way. Why is that?"

Using your imagination, with no effort at all, pretend you are twice as confident as you've ever been before. With each breath bring more of the feeling of confidence to you. Expand into a naturally confident state of being, just because you want to. Overachievers, pretend someone who doubts you walks into the room, and stay completely confident just the same.

9. clear the air. Now let's clear our air to soar. For the next twenty-four hours, letting lightness be your guide, make your air:

- **TENSION-FREE:** When tension arises, handle it immediately. This means talk it out, walk it out, and ask for clarification as need be.
- **NEGATIVITY-FREE:** Yes, we can complain about something without the whine, using a natural voice, showing a clarity of purpose. Better yet, we can ask for specifically what we need for clear, decisive, forward movement.
- **ASSUMPTION-FREE:** Ask, rather than assume, to ensure squeaky clean air. The most skilled executives I know ask the simplest questions that everyone else has, too, but holds back, assuming they should already know the answers. Start at ground zero and build up from there.
- **EXAGGERATION-FREE:** Exaggerations can leave a residue in a room, smelling a bit less than true and hinting that a normal-sized world is less than acceptable. Try being more precise with your statements, even when you're trying to stir up someone else's energy, and see if it feels more light.
- **HONESTY-FULL:** How refreshing to find a person who will tell you about that piece of lettuce in your teeth, the mascara smear under your eye, the fly that's unzipped, or put words to describe the elephant that's in the room. Clean air has to be honesty-full.
- **LAUGHTER-FULL:** If we can see the humor in something and give it a good belly laugh, the air instantly clears.

At first glance, these may seem like rules to remember, but they're not—they're "energy to follow." It's a big difference. You can *feel* tension in your body. You can *feel* when you puff yourself up to exaggerate. You can *feel* the weight of secrets, assumptions, *scribble here . . .*

and white lies. I'm just putting words to these feelings and asking that for the next twenty-four hours, whenever you feel these things, you make a lighter choice. Then you'll feel the lift.

10. flying to altitude. Let's work our energetic muscles and build some nice altitude using our subtle "open" and "closed" states—contract, expand, contract, expand . . . *fly.* If you find yourself getting distracted by your brain, put earplugs in.

- **CREATIVE OUTLETS.** Pretend you are tired at the end of the day. Then pick up your favorite evening thing to do, your creative outlet—be it cooking, exercising, art, reading, playing with the kids, sex, or a hobby or two. Feel yourself relax and re-expand.

- **THE FIRST TEN.** Write down in the margin the names of the last ten people you interacted with: day care workers, grocery clerks, colleagues, family, friends, etc. Then circle the ones who are the most positive, around whom you don't have to guard yourself against anything.

- **ATTENTION-GRABBER 1.** Imagine you're in the military and the top dog comes into the room. Someone says, *"Ten hut!!!"* and you stand at attention. The top dog responds *"At ease,"* and you relax again, though not quite as fully as you were before he walked in. Repeat.

- **ATTENTION-GRABBER 2.** Pretend you're single, with a group of single friends complaining about things, perhaps sloppily dressed, and definitely dragging at the end of the day. Then an oh-so-eligible-and-gorgeous gal or guy sits in the empty chair. Feel how quickly you rebound.

- **IT'S THE PHONE!** Write down the names of ten people you get phone calls from. Any ten will do. Then put them in order of the "lift" or "drop" you normally feel after hearing their voice on the other end of the line.

- **GENEROSITY.** Put both a mental- and heart-picture to: Open-hearted generosity. Tight-fisted stinginess. Giving yourself a break. Beating yourself up. Generosity with an agenda. Gifts that have strings. Not spending much at all, but being entirely open to the world.

- **WHITE LIES.** Catch yourself in your next white lie, the teeniest, tiniest one will do, something you're just pretending is true. Then toss it away, not even bothering to tell another soul. This truth is strictly for you.

- **CLOSING TIME.** Think of someone you feel is "closed." Now imagine him or her opening up wide.

- **GOOD TIMING.** On a small piece of paper, write down one thing that you want and are getting impatient waiting for. Then tuck the piece of paper away in your favorite jar or drawer. Open for its answer to come to you. Toss logic away and really open wide.

11. enjoy the view. Once you've reached soaring altitude, your perspective will astound you. Sometime this week, simulate the view that you'd have during a nice solid soar. Go find a place with a great view and hang out there for a while.

12. feel the wind. Let's bring our full attention to the wind of inspiration that's dancing at our door. Open your senses to feel the following: Wind instruments such as clarinets and flutes. The whoosh when a parachute fills. Wind surfers jumping the waves. Windfalls filling investment accounts. Windmills channeling energy for human use. Humans using wind sprints to build their quads. Wind chimes that sing to you each morning. Windsocks that dance in the breeze. Allow yourself to open to the generosity of the wind, and feel a warm thermal rising up to support you.

13. movement is mandatory, a quickie. Breathe three times in and out. One . . . two . . . three. Then, with or without shoes, as you prefer, start wiggling your toes for a count of ten to loosen yourself up.

14. loveliness. Breathe in the memory of something or someone you love. Or life in general. Let it fill every cell of your being.

15. stop flapping and yakking. Are you ready to soar through today? Your energetic muscles are trained. You're at altitude. You feel the wind as a supportive force. The time is now! Set that internal switch to "ease" for the rest of the day. Make any duties, deadlines, and pleasures as anxiety-free as they can possibly be. Begin by breezing through the rest of these exercises.

permission to soar

flipping the switch

In the middle of finals week, my friend Georgia wrote me an e-mail.

"This morning I was in that strange place where I felt like I was on the ocean, an angry ocean. And of course, like everyone else, my first instinct was to paddle really hard. But I knew deep down that panicking would only make the situation worse. All I needed to do was relax, breathe, release my tension . . . then roll over and float on my back.

"So I gave myself permission and floated *all* day today. Not quite here. Not quite there. Not looking for shore. Not giving a flying *'you-know-what'* about who's keeping score or who's laughing at my refusal to swim. I literally detached from the dramatic hubbub, the frenzied energy that was trying to draw me in. I thought of other things . . . and nothing at the same time. I thought of the 'me' that I am and the 'me' that I want to be. The 'me' that I sometimes project for others to see didn't exist today, and I love that. I carved out a free space and called a time out.

"Ironically, I still did all of the things that I was sup-posed to do. The world didn't stop turning. And the rain didn't make me sad. I didn't have to physically remove myself from the world. I didn't have to overeat or underestimate myself to make it happen. I just cut off that switch that makes living tough. That one that measures expectancy against actual achievement. That one that counts how many M & M's you eat each week. Thanks for the reminder, Sally. I wish you could remind everyone to shut off their switch now and then, to rethink their day. It really works wonders."

16. open, open, open wide. Did you ever see that department store ad where a lady is waiting in the pre-dawn darkness for the store to open and the sale to begin? In a kind of magic incantation, she throws her fingers out wide three times, palms to the glass, looking at all the wonders that lay just out of her reach, crying, *"Open, open, open!"* in rhythm with her movement. It's a feeling that many of us can identify with—having something so close we can practically taste it . . . but yet so far away.

Let's take that actress's lead and practice opening wide to the possibility of what life has in store.

- **FRESH AIR.** If it's comfortable, open the windows—*wide.*
- **A GOOD START.** Write a list in the margin of things that, even blindfolded, you know how to do.
- **HOWDY DOODY.** Say hi to three neighbors, kids, or strangers today.
- **FIRST CHILDHOOD FRIEND.** Call in the breeze that carries the memory of your first childhood friend.

- **SOUTHERN COMFORT.** Think about your favorite pair of socks and how comfy your feet feel when you put them on.

- **A NATURAL HIGH.** Breathe four nice fresh breaths of mountain, sea, city, and country air in . . . from wherever you are reading this right now.

- **LOOSEN THOSE LIPS.** Write down the names of five people that you can be "open" with—yes, hairdressers, bartenders, and complete strangers count.

- **THE WRITE STUFF.** Agnes always uses a typewriter so her hands are opened wide as she writes. Closing her hand around a pen just wouldn't invite the same creativity, she claims. Pretend that you're writing something right now. Feel the flow out of your open fingertips and onto the page.

- **FREE FLOW.** Dance around the room, moving your arms, legs, and hips precisely as *they* want to move *you.*

- **TRAVEL SOMEWHERE NEW.** Whether across the world or town, or in your rich imagination, take a trip.

- **SPARE NO EXPENSE.** If you're the type who writes $5 checks to charity, stretch those wings and experience writing a check for $25. Those $100 check writers, try $1,000. Check writers of $100,000, go for a cool mil. Open.

- **STRETCH YOUR LIMITS.** Do something wonderful for yourself, bigger than you've ever done before. Make it really, really, really big (whatever "really big" means to you).

17. it's no exaggeration. At first, you may have thought that the lift you'd feel from a good soar would come from an exaggeration, a puffing up, or from putting someone else down. The power to soar actually comes from thinking big while being real, without exaggerating at all. For example, if I were to say that I wanted to be president of the United States one day, it would be a lie—no power in it

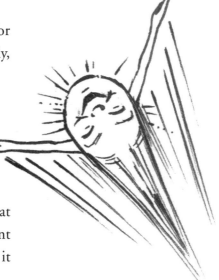

at all. But to change the world's view that powerful half of one degree? Count me in. I'm there. Five hundred trillion horses couldn't stop me. And that's no fib.

Without exaggerating even slightly, but with thinking really, really, really big, is there one thing that pops to mind that you really, really, really want to do, say, or be?

18. happy hour. Most of us naturally have a few minutes between the time that we first awaken and actually get out of bed. Many of us use this time to tighten a vise grip firmly around our to-do lists. Why not use these precious minutes to *open wide* instead? Open that mind, let a gentle breeze flow through, stretching your energetic muscles at the start of each day. Enjoy the lift it brings.

You may notice that if you have something that's plugging your pipes, corking your bottle, or blocking the wind, you can feel a sense of irritation or resistance when you try this exercise. If so, look for what's lying underneath it, let the thought gently rise up and reveal itself to you. Be gentle, keep open, and soon you'll be enjoying daily Happy Hours, too.

Overachievers, add a nice glass of your favorite freshly squeezed fruit juice.

wrap-up

Soaring has many faces. One can soar through a series of complicated tasks or through the most mundane routine. It's an attitude, an opportunity, a choice. At its core is the willingness to open fully to life. And the secret to its power, to circumventing the vulnerability that is often associated with opening yourself wide, is to stay connected to how you really, really, really feel inside. Let this inner connection guide your outer movements. The more honest your connection, the more confident and flexible you are. The more honest your connection, the easier your flight. The more honest your connection, the more brilliant your natural shine.

step 8, glow

GOAL: **PARTNER WITH YOUR INNER PASSIONS.** *In this step we are moved—uncontrollably, undeniably, and irresistibly—by our inner passion. All 10,000 watts of it. We find it, then make it real, from the inside out. The more parts of ourselves we let out, the bigger our glow. The bigger our glow, the greater our vitality. To glow is our most relaxed, natural, simple, and powerful state of being.*

Who are you? What do you love to do? What feeds you? What stokes your inner flame? We're speaking here beyond potato chips and hot dogs, past eggplant and caviar . . . to the real you, and your favorite soul food.

In Glow (Step 8), all of the individual steps and isolated movements we've been experiencing are brought together into one fluid motion. The disassembly gets reassembled into one glorious you. No longer do we view a contraction as separate from an expansion, or a closure as distinct from an opening. The two join together to form a pulse, a breath, the pumping of a heart. Antagonists partner with protagonists to create wonderful, dramatic plots for a play. Dark colors and light ones splash themselves on the same canvases to create beautiful scenes. Loud notes partner with soft ones, punctuated with silence, to form a symphony.

As my friend Agnes enjoys reminding me, in all art forms opposites are harmonized, made seamless, brought together in a most intriguing and pleasurable way. In this step we bring being human to an art form, discovering that our glow burns brightest when each part of our real selves is free to come out.

When whole, our soul integrates with each of our movements and begins moving us playfully and mysteriously along. Life becomes less of a chore and more of a dance, a puzzle, a play. Simply noticing a roadblock often sends it on its way. Resistance lessens. Perspectives broaden. Opportunities appear. We learn to sense when to reach inside for answers and when to reach out, when to take action and when to powerfully wait. The push-pull of the soul becomes more delicate, a friend that whispers in our ear. A healthy vitality powers us, and a luminous glow brightens our cells.

The glow is a gentle force that is released when our insides are gracefully out there for all to enjoy. It's powered by our passions but is brightest when we are most relaxed and warm. It flows with simple treasures but doesn't care about the size of the house we live in. It's who you are. It's where your flavor is. Our glow moves us like a dancer across the floor. Think Ginger. Think Fred. Think flow. Think *glow*.

The glow is a gentle force that is released when our insides are gracefully out there for all to enjoy.

a dream come true

As soon as I awoke, without the benefit of hindsight, I knew that the dream I'd had would change the way I approached life. It marked the end of an old phase and the start of something very new. It happened a few weeks after leaving my job.

"In my dream I was at the office—my *old* office, I should say," I told Jessica. "There was gunfire everywhere. The new managers were armed with long rifles like people in old Westerns. But instead of shooting their way out of a saloon when a card game went bad, they were shooting their way into our company.

"Not surprisingly, I was trying to protect the team. I would gently nudge them one way or the other, or cause a distraction so a team member would walk a few feet in a different direction, barely missing a bullet. Sometimes I would call a meeting so an ambush would be prevented. Against all odds, I was single-handedly taking on the enemy."

Jessica stirred uncomfortably in her chair, not noticing the twinkle in my eye.

"Then I saw one of our junior managers, our shining star, moving directly into the line of fire," I continued. "I could have saved her. I had the time. But in the split second I'd had to act, I made the conscious choice not to.

"Then the gunman, shocked at landing this grand prize, moved his large rifle in my direction. I stood there calmly as he aimed his gun and shot. Everything switched to slow motion as I bent down to the left to make sure the bullet wound would be fatal. I remember being disgusted that they couldn't even kill me cleanly without my help.

"Soon a second shot rang out and hit me higher in the chest. *'So they would have killed me after all,'* I thought, smiling at their cunning. *'I didn't have to help.'*"

Jessica was even more nervous now, but this time I let her see that I was anything but agitated at the experience of my metaphoric death.

"I felt myself floating effortlessly down, down, down, past layer after layer of . . . earth, I think . . . like a feather would fall from a bird in flight, but with more momentum. I landed peacefully at what felt like the center of the earth, and met another person from my office there. He smiled knowingly at me. Silently we held each other in a long, firm embrace until tears welled up from what seemed like the deepest part of our beings, our communication being more perfect and complete in that moment than at any time or with anyone before. We were being cleansed from the inside out . . . tensions gone, fears removed, a peace filling us. Marvelous.

"I awoke from the dream with a start, shocked that my dream's tears had made their way to my very own pillow. *Real tears.* My inner and outer worlds were one, my innermost self having found a clear path to the surface—tangible, indisputable, undeniable, for everyone to see."

Jessica responded with her smile rather than words.

"Freeing could be one word to use," I continued. "Or authentic. But even that seems a bit staid. Really, really *connected* and really, really *real* and really, really *relieved* that the fight was finally over is about the best I can do to describe this one. I don't mean just the physical fight with the new parent company, either. And I don't mean the twenty-four-hour-a-day factory grind. It feels much bigger than that— *HUGE, in fact.* I've given up the fight, Jessica, my old way of approaching life. A new option has appeared. A huge boulder's been kicked off the path from my inner soul to the outer world. I can be *me* now, Jessica. I'm free to be *me!*"

Jessica's soul chose that moment to water her eyes, making tearstains on her shirt to match those on my pillow. I felt my clarity and vitality crank itself up to all-time highs and my ability to fake, pretend, or deceive myself notch down by an equal amount. And my soul? It just glowed.

do, be, create

What if our souls could come out to play and rule every minute of every day? I'm not talking go-with-the-flow hippy style, I'm talking *responsibly*—with trained muscles, an objective view, power, and grace. With a superhighway in place from our most soulful selves to the world and back again, what would our days look like? So "out there," exposed, open, unguarded, how would we be?

he thought it couldn't happen

a holiday miracle

A month before I left my old factory, not long after our merger had gone into effect, our newest customer threw us a party, grateful that we'd kept their production lines running during a critical time. Two hundred sixty-five team members filled the Seattle Space Needle's private banquet floor. Christmas carolers, gaily-decorated tables, and Santa Claus greeted us. Several ladies from the factory floor put on ball gowns and old bridesmaid dresses for the occasion. It was quite an affair.

When my new boss from the multinational-conglomerate arrived, he was in shock. "I thought there were going to be six or eight of us," he said, obviously not realizing that our customer had hired a small fleet of buses to bring the whole group to the center of town. "I've never heard of a customer doing such a thing."

His mind struggled to find a rational explanation for something only a heart could feel. Miracles didn't exist in his world. But I delighted in the fact that when hearts were opened and inner fires ablaze, miracles always, always, always appeared.

Flexible and creative is my simple answer. We simply wouldn't be able to stop ourselves. Once we get used to living "open-souled," our passions will pop right out. Nothing else will hold our interest for long. We'll tell people what's on our minds without trying to convince them of anything. We'll show an inner confidence with a calm, strong edge. We'll lose our self-consciousness and keep our self-respect. Rushing will become less useful to us, though we'll go for what we care about at full speed. The rest we'll happily leave to someone else. Prejudice and mental blocks will naturally melt away.

We can be more true to ourselves, truly we can. We can stop buying presents because we have to, and start giving people things because it feels good. We can stop accepting invitations that we're anything less than thrilled to receive, and start doing the things that make us thrilled to be alive. We can leave relationships we're just clinging to, and start doing what really matters to us in life. We can quit jobs that require us to fake it, stuff it, or dim our bulbs in any way. We can take the energy of any anger, irritation, or annoyance we're feeling and use it to soar, transforming our jobs, homes, and relationships into ones that are right for us. We can combine individual passions and create as a non-competitive, well-oiled team.

Remember in the first chapter when I talked about constructively "destructive" and constructively "constructive" passions? One is the punch-through passion that breaks down barriers. The other is its more gentle cousin that bubbles up like a fountain, pulling us out of the bed in the morning to get a jumpstart on the day. In this step we're going to play with those two feisty friends, seek them out in others, as well as dig them up and out of ourselves.

You can think of my real-tears-on-the-pillow dream as being the flow of this deeper, constructive passion finding a clear path out. You see, I'd already "self-destructed," popped my cork, so to speak, when I left my old company, said good-bye to the fight-the-good-fight world, and followed my inner voice into the new. This created a wind tunnel for my soul's energy to channel through. Drops from the ocean of my soul, once buried down, down, down inside of me made it up, up, up through this tunnel, and past the surface of my skin to the linen of my pillowcase. I was hidden no more. And I didn't mind one bit that my soul's expression took the form of ancient tears.

When our corks have popped, our inner channels set in a safe-and-fully-open position, when we are confident that, yes, many things will rock us, but *nothing* will keep us down for long . . . when that moment arrives, our souls have an unencumbered path out. Our engines are stoked. Our fires are lit. And follow our inner passions, we must. Do, be, create.

I know, I know, many of you are saying *"But I don't know what my passion is . . . I'm not creative . . . I'm not an artist . . . She'd better not ask me to pick up a paintbrush or start singing—no way!"* Don't worry. I want for you only what you want for yourself. I'm not necessarily talking about being creative in the artistic sense. Creativity has many faces. It can take the form of the words we speak, ideas we bring to the dining and/or conference room tables, meals we cook, relationships we build, children we raise, dreams we have, hobbies we love, classes we teach, parties we throw, perspectives we hold, or projects we complete. We are born to create—passionately.

I have yet to meet a person who isn't capable of creating a fully satisfying life. I've met many people who aren't willing to do so or who don't think they can, but that's a different story. And I suspect that since you're reading the final chapter of this book, you are quite *ready, willing, and able (all three!).* In fact, I'd bet on it.

Each of us has a voice to share and a uniqueness to express, with a passion at its base. But too often people fear that being passionate about something can make them different from the rest. Why not look at it, instead, as each person bringing a unique contribution to the table—something big, little, or in between? It may not be a grandiose gift, per se, but one is no more powerful than the other. Just the unique way we look at the world may open someone else's eyes, if we only had the courage to speak it, if we only had the courage to try.

And try, we must. Being our whole selves is not our right, it's our responsibility.

I once heard an art critic say that artists are not just different, they are *outside* of society. They scare people when they bring new ideas to light. They terrify us, he continued to say, by asking us to open our consciousness to a new perspective, a new combination of colors or words, a new idea that might destroy the world as we know it, or present a new way of being.

I couldn't argue with him. The desire to fit in often wins out. But that world is so bland, boring, and small to me.

If we see someone shining, we either run like hell . . . or gravitate to the light, greedily at times, and equally confident that a candle loses none of its light by lighting another, thrilled at the companionship, challenge, and opportunity it brings.

Those of us labeled *artist, entrepreneur, inventor, instigator, risktaker, ringleader, passionate, peculiar, genuine, warm, feisty, fresh, different, difficult, rambunctious, rabble-rouser, outspoken, curious, strikingly honest, or alive* are the ones I want to hang around. They open me wide. The others too often resist all but the most controllable changes, the guaranteed solutions, or the safest paths.

If we see someone shining, we either run like hell . . . or gravitate to the light, greedily at times, and equally confident that a candle loses none of its light by lighting another, thrilled at the companionship, challenge, and opportunity it brings.

Sitting there in the auditorium that day, the art critic's sentiments stirring up feelings of my own, a split-second-open-close choice presented itself. I could make my next move a relatively safe one, or go even another step further out on that limb. I think you know what I decided. Competitiveness, jealousy, and fear took a backseat that day. I am going for passion, for creation, for the new, no matter what! I want to hang with the "lit" crowd. I want to be surrounded by positivity in every single thing I do. I want movement, expression, freedom, and space. I want to break through barriers I don't even feel yet, but sense are yet to come. I want to be out of all boxes. And my soul wants to come in, to be a part of every big, small, and medium-sized decision that I face.

coming to my senses

The last story I'm going to leave you with is the creation of this book. As with everything else I've written here, interpret it metaphorically—less as a first-time author drama, and more as the unfolding of two souls (both mine and the book's). Feel the various stages that the manuscript went through—from the initial seventy-five-page-boxed-up-tight-super-focused version to the overly-expanded-give-it-all-I've-got-exaggerated-in-the-other-direction version to the final draft that you are reading right now. See if you can spot the moment when the struggle ended and the book's soul was born, with me as its partner, mother, and friend.

A publisher told me once that all first books are autobiographical in nature—either overtly so (like this one) or disguised in some way. It made sense to me. Once one's uniqueness begins to boil and bubble, it needs a focus to concentrate its energy and send any cork that's been plugging it sky high. The publisher then added that once that first book is out ("behind you" were her actual words, punctuated by an ill-disguised, bored sigh), the author is then free to do anything. Absolutely anything. I sure hope she's right.

When I began this book, as you may recall, I was on vacation in Arizona, getting a much-needed break from the chaos of our company's impending merger. Over the next weeks, my exhaustion left as my inner drive to teach began to build. I was on a mission, waking up at 5:00 A.M. before heading to the office, packaging my story in a tight seventy-five-page box. When I sent the draft to a handful of close friends to review, I found myself quite nervous at how they would take this window into a side of me that not even they knew.

The reviews were good. A friend arranged for a meeting with a publisher in New York. Serendipity was on my side.

The editor told me to keep the personal story format, but open and expand it—wider than wide. *"This isn't just for chronic fatigue sufferers,"* she said with a smile. *"It's for the overachiever in all of us, the part unsatisfied with life's ride. Show us how you managed your energy, introduce us to your friends. There are millions of people who want more energy in their days."*

For three and a half months I contentedly typed away, diving into my soul, reliving each up and down. The new 450-page draft finished, back to the publisher it went. But right there it stayed, not making it to print.

Dejected and confused, I wasn't sure what to do. In the spirit of "power-waiting," I stopped doing anything at all and invited the next step *to come to me*, which it did. I began to teach, initially as a sidekick to a friend. I spoke at health spas, college campuses, and companies. Exposing myself to a huge slice of life, I circled the globe, expanding my view.

power-wait

the power of pregnancy

Being happily pregnant as I write these words, I can tell you that waiting is not for wimps. It has real power. From the single conception that sets the ball in motion, the time before a birth allows much movement to happen. The couple gets used to the idea of being parents. The nursery gets put together. Exuberance builds. The unexpected can enter in many, many ways—some with "good" labels, others with "bad." And if the baby's like ours, she'll appear in people's dreams—playing with them at night, having lively conversations.

Let's coin a new term, "power-wait," and change waiting's image from its current passive and meager place. Let's make waiting active, vibrant, hopeful, open, and alive. It's a great use for our radar, those eyes in the back of our heads.

If you don't know what you want, if you do but feel it's just out of reach, the old way of handling this was to rush, force, plan, manipulate, and control it into being. The new way is to keep your long-term vision crystal clear, take just the steps that lie directly in front of you, then power-wait until the next move appears. An ocean liner, after all, takes some time to change course.

How does power-waiting differ from being stuck, you ask? Hugely. Feel it. Pretend you're stuck—closed, defensive, sad, back-to-the-wall, crumbled, scared. A power-wait position is wide open, expectant, trusting, and clear. Sure, you can also feel timid, annoyed, or impatient around the edges, with a sprinkling of fear. But on balance, your openness wins, and puts the power in your wait.

How many times have we heard about a person giving up on something they've been trying so hard to have or do (pushing, shoving, clawing, or clinging to), then suddenly for that same something to walk right on in? A power-wait works with this same kind of open energy.

Americans are taught to do, know, and achieve. Freedom, liberty, diversity, and opportunity for all. Go after that dream! Other cultures are more comfortable with the passage of time. Italian men can stay home without comment until long past age thirty-five. Three-months' notice is common there when leaving a job. So if you need help with the rough edges that power-waiting can stir up, go rent a sleepy foreign film for a night.

About a year into this, with my manuscript collecting dust back at home, a woman patiently waited for the lecture hall to clear so she could talk to me one-on-one. Yes, my fairy tale came full circle that day, as this Hollywood producer introduced me to a literary agent who simply loved my book.

A framework for the soul's movement, the dance of life, is what I sought. And I couldn't cut it into pieces. It had to stay whole to be right.

But I soon fell into a downward spiral as rejection letters from potential publishers started coming in. When all hope had nearly gone, a single gentle breeze remained, bringing with it the voice of the very last publisher on the list.

"You are trying too hard," she said. *"The answer is easier than you may think. I can feel a jewel in there. It's just buried a bit. Inspire the public with your personal story, then give them the steps, a way to do it themselves. There's a reason there are so many ten- and twelve-step self-help books."*

A framework for the soul's movement, the dance of life, is what I sought. And I couldn't cut it into pieces. It had to stay whole to be right. A full year later, on a particularly windy February day, the first word of the new manuscript came out. Some steps were easy, the ones I'd been teaching for years. But some steps were elusive, dodging my search to express them in words.

Then with a colleague's assistance, a warm voice on the e-line, my inner connection was fortified, my direction set. Entire chapters I'd written were chipped off my rough diamond, recognized as dead ends. New adjectives were born, words and ideas split apart to cut new facets out of the old. Therapy helps, I heard myself say, but it can leave you dry, with excuses and blame. How do we really go forward, how do we make that big leap? What are the feeling-based signals that can show us the way? I searched for only the truest sensations to use as a guide, the answer to how to bring passion to life.

One day my colleague suggested that I throw away even more and reach way, way out into the new. *"Pretend your book is still being read one hundred years from now,"* she teased. *"Think big and bigger yet. Really, really, really stretch."*

That did it. The lid on my box exploded, sending both me and the book sky-high. We both began to fly. Over one hundred pages came out of me in one short October week. I was surfing a wave, steadily and skillfully, occasionally and playfully thrown off balance by its force. During those times, about an hour or two after having finished for the day, I'd feel raw, exposed, shaky—buck naked in the wind. This became my signature, my indication, my sign, that I'd touched the book's power, that I'd found its sweet spot.

What was most interesting about writing the final steps for the book was that I couldn't write them alone. The wind through the manuscript's pages was simply too strong for one person to hold. Friends and I literally read the text out loud to one another.

The book had come alive. It was an organic being. A way out had finally been found for what wanted to be said. I discovered who I was and what I wanted to say. If I can do this for myself, you can do it, too.

let the games begin: For the rest of this chapter (and for the rest of our lives), let's walk around like we all have 10,000 watt shines, opened so wide that all options lie before us and prejudices cease to exist. Limits are old news, dreams are in. "Ease" has four letters but isn't considered a dirty word. There are plenty of hours to the day. Laughter surrounds us. Every need is met. Now let's see what vital energy this kind of attitude can release. Whether there's a passion tickling your funny bone right now or you're unsure what your unique slant on life really is, the games in our playground will have something for you. So if you're ready, let the games begin!

changes won't scare you anymore.

Closed boxes, stagnancy, insincerity, and inflexibility will. Toe stubs and pebbles in one's path have been reported to carry an annoyance factor previously associated with dating rejections, self-hatred, and pink slips. "Faking it" in any way whatsoever literally hurts. Mid-course corrections, confrontations, and dance lessons bring a rush of fresh energy instead of dread. Surprisingly, a lower-than-average impatience with people who don't operate in the same way was reported, likely a result of a broad perspective being firmly in place. Most people surveyed reported that their incidence of saying "No" was markedly increased, while "Yes" responses were on a decline. The number of "HELL, YES!" responses shouted from rooftops, however, was at an all-time high.

1. look back. Which steps were the most natural, easiest for you? Which were the hardest for you to get through? Steps 3 and 7 are the ones I too easily forget—stepping-into-the-shining-light and giving-up-the-fight. Dog ear any steps that you may want to refer back to. Overachievers, scribble why in the margins.

2. movement is mandatory. Let's warm up for life's dance, shall we? Stretch your arms up high, then wide. Take a big breath in, and let a bigger one out. Now, bring to mind your absolute, positive biggest fans—be they your mother, therapist, boss, colleagues, or friends. Open your heart and let them even more deeply in. Overachievers, take this opportunity to get rid of just one person, activity, or thing that isn't completely, absolutely, in-line with the "you" that you are right now. Travel light.

3. outer glow. Step 6's dance partner is pain, working with that punch, that inner gut-wrenching, doubled-over contraction. Step 7's partner is pleasure, opening to its wave with grace and ease, taking the "hard" out of work. Step 8's partner is passion, that inner engine and feisty fuel. Everyone has at least one passion inside. And believe it or not, everyone knows exactly what his or her passions are. It's just that they can be either too close to see, too powerful to embrace, or too long-ignored to locate.

Let's start our passionate search by looking outside ourselves first. Which people would you put on the top of the passion list—a permanent glow in place, unshakable in their vision (whether simple or grandiose), marching to the beat of their own drummer, warm, flexible, open, and confident? Perhaps they have the kind of passion that punches through obstacles, the say-it-like-it-is-take-no-prisoners kind. Or the kind that bubbles up silently from the inside, covering those canvases, filling those pages, making those words riveting. Or the kind that beams of freshness, of wide-open hearts, and comfort in their very own skin, with no specific external form at all, but whose glow is infectious just the same.

Do you know even one person who's got "the glow?"

4. inner glow, passion with a punch. Now that we're warmed up, let's flip around and look at our very own inner passions, starting with the constructively "destructive" kind. When the soul begins to stir, if it doesn't have enough room to move, it can build up a pressure strong enough to rival Old Faithful. This is the passion with an angry edge, a pent-up hunger, a force powerful enough to destroy the most burdensome of barriers, stage protests, change laws, and leap tall buildings in a single bound. Mismanaged, this passion fuels explosions, violence, and acting out. Well-managed, it supports us to break free, tell the truth, and take a stand. "Destructive" passion is found in the moment after the hopelessness fades and the instant before words jump out of our mouth. This passion-with-a-punch breaks through the layers of tradition, fear, or habit that cover the heart, exposing its prize, and opening the soul's wings to spread wide.

Identify up to five punch-through passionate moments you've had. Were they graceful or not? Afterwards, did a vulnerable feeling arise?

5. inner glow, let your deepest passion out. Constructively "constructive" passion is the energy that bubbles up from the bottom of your soul, bringing creativity in its wake. It's a natural force, very much alive, and kicks you out of bed in the morning, giving you an enthusiasm that you don't have to work yourself up for. Like its punchy cousin, constructive passion can also blow the top off a volcano, even though it's often tame and sweet. Bubbly passion can keep you up at night, put thoughts in your head all day, demand your attention over all else, and make your conversations a little lop-sided. You're not in control of your life anymore. You're in a partnership.

Partnering with your passion rarely has making money as its goal, though making lots of money can be a natural result. Passion is like a shoe that really fits. It's an energy spring that moves you.

Sometimes we need to get a distance from our routine, from how we've been viewing ourselves, for our passion to pop out. When I was writing this book, I cancelled all speaking engagements for an entire year so I could distance myself from the old words I'd been using, and make room for fresh ones to appear.

Will you need a year, too, I can hear you asking? Probably not. I had that hard Sicilian head, overly-abundant brain, and a lot of momentum to shift. Heck, one good inspirational moment is all it really takes. So open, open, open . . . feel that trickle (or geyser!) rise up . . . and let its movement move you. Movement is what passion's all about.

Remember, this is another feeling exercise. It's not a thinking thing. After you do the warm-up, find the angles that most intrigue you from the list below, and do as many as you'd like. The more relaxed you are, the better. It's not a deep sea dive we're going for here, no heavy excavation work. It's an awakening.

passionate warm-up

Let's get our energetic muscles nicely warmed-up for this passionate exercise.

- **HEARTFELT.** As you read these words, coordinate them with your breath. Open your heart and chest wide as you breathe in, then close them. Open, then close. Do this several more times to really loosen you up. Let your breath naturally follow along. Open your heart, close your heart. Open, close . . . open, close. Now take a deep breath, and ask that heart to stay in a fully-open position for the rest of this chapter.

> - **RELAX AND EXPAND.** Let's get into our most powerful position—completely relaxed and expanded. Imagine the best vacation place anywhere in the world, whatever "best" means to you. Get a picture of it in your mind, put its taste on your lips, let its fragrance linger around you, and imagine its sound filling the air. Then put yourself into the scene. Breathe it in. Wiggle your toes. Yes, you're on vacation. You're doing exactly what you want to be doing. Perfect.

Feel those passion bubbles rise:

- **OPEN UP.** Take a journey through your heart and into your soul, feel your passion, ride its bubbles out, then ask them what they love to do. Okay, okay, if you're not quite up for this one, there are plenty of other facets of the passion diamond from which to choose.

- **WHAT DO YOU LOVE TO DO?** Write it down. Yes, even the teeniest, tiniest things count, like licking ice cream cones. Remember this is a feeling thing. Just open and let your most fun words flow out.

- **WHAT IT ISN'T.** Maybe you'd prefer to get those passion juices flowing by writing down what your passion *is not,* the things you couldn't care less about. You may be surprised at your clarity here.

- **JUICE BAR.** Perhaps these words will tempt you—what stirs your juices, turns you on, lights your fire, and burns your desire? What propels you out the door without so much as a backwards glance? Again, you can write a list of these things, or relax with them under a big blue sky.

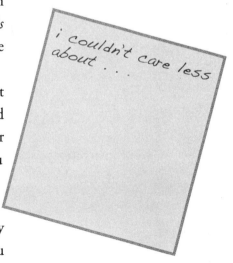

- **ANNOYANCES.** Perhaps the perspective that will pry open your passion is to look at what really annoys you and see if a hint of your passion lies beneath it.

these light my fire!

how annoying!. . .

- **ASK SOMEONE ELSE.** But be extremely careful who you pick for this advice. Pick someone wise, an astute observer who both gets you and would never dream of criticizing, downplaying, manipulating, influencing, or having even the teeniest doubt.

- **LISTEN TO YOURSELF.** As you talk to that wise someone, the words that describe your passion might just pop out.

- **YOUR TONE MAY TELL.** Notice the tone of your voice. When you say your passion out loud, your voice will reflect its power. Try the reverse and say someone else's passion—you'll feel the difference in your vocal cords. Overachievers, listen to other people's voices as they speak about things they're passionate about, compared to things they really don't care much about at all. Feel the difference.

- **WHEN WE WERE FOUR.** Passion often reveals itself at a very young age. Remember back to your early childhood and the things that mattered most to you, what intrigued you, and the questions you asked. Either talk them out or write them down.

- **REGRETFUL.** Pretending you might die tomorrow, what would you look back and regret not having done?

- **LIMITLESS, TIMELESS, EFFORTLESS.** Pretend you are starting over again and have all the time in the world, as well as the limitless enthusiasm of others to support you. What would you want to do?

- **SELF-CREATED ASSIGNMENTS.** Look back at the things you've done for the office, charity, hobbies, or home, that were entirely your idea to do.

- **LIFE-LONG FASCINATIONS.** What's yours?

- **WHEN TIME FLIES.** Is there something that you can do for hours and it not seem to tire you? That makes time fly?

let your deepest passions out!

pick your approach and fill that page!

what and who i appreciate . . .

6. we're done with the disassembly, it's time to say YES!

- **WHAT AND WHO DO YOU REALLY, REALLY, REALLY APPRECIATE?** Without thinking at all, write a list down the margin of this page.

- **WHAT DO YOU REALLY, REALLY, REALLY WANT?** Not just a yes, but a *"Hell, yes!"* is what we are going for here. An 11 on a scale of one to ten. The thing wild horses couldn't keep you away from (even if you get scared and try to talk yourself out of it two seconds later!). You know it'll feed you and make your heart soar. So dream. Toss those limits and logic away.

  Oops, I can feel some of you saying, *"But dare I dream again? My hopes have been dashed so many times."* I can't argue with this. I've been there, too. But you can either accept your life as it is today—*sincerely*—or open yourself to the possibility that an even more fulfilling one exists. A shift usually takes but one half of one degree: the dropping of a routine, the opening of a heart or mind, or one small, decisive forward step. Either way it's your choice: stretch yourself or stay put.

  "But I don't know what I want," I can hear you saying now. For now pick something small. Maybe a first date rather than a marriage, a new outfit rather than a whole new shape, an understanding reached with that cantankerous client rather than a whole new career. Or it could be less tangible, something driven from your inner world, like a secret revealed, the right words found, an internal peace felt, or a relief for those racing thoughts in your head. Pick one thing you really want. That's it.

Overachievers, to confirm that this choice is what you really, really, really want, move your attention from those big, beautiful brains right down to your hearts. Put both hands there in a pledge of allegiance to yourself. Ask your heart if it's satisfied with your choice.

Right now, everyone, even if you think you "failed" this exercise, move on to the next. Because even if you don't know *what* you really want, you may have an inkling *with whom.*

- **WHO DO YOU REALLY, REALLY, REALLY WANT TO DO IT WITH?** Birds often soar alone, but I've never met a person who has, particularly at the start of something new. That's a delicate time when it's best not to have a pessimist in sight. This doesn't mean surround yourself with "yes men," patsies, or wimps. I'm talking about people with opinions with whom you can banter back and forth. Being direct and clear is actually more polite than politeness could ever be. You're looking for flying partners you really trust, who sport one face, not two. When they say yes, they really mean it. And when they say no, there's a reassurance in that, too. The connection is felt, the trust is secure, and a confidence is born from pure honesty.

  A man asked me once what I'd do with a crusty, stuck company like his. "Absolutely nothing," I replied. If someone at the top doesn't get it, you wouldn't find me there. There are plenty of people and companies that are ripe to soar on creativity and recognize the value of the genuinely imperfect human being.

For this exercise, identify which people (or companies) you want to say *"Hell, yes!"* to. Note that it's less of putting the rest of your colleagues and friends *out* a circle or two, and more of bringing your selective few *even farther in*.

- **WHAT STEP IS REALLY, REALLY, REALLY NEXT?** We're looking for a single action item here—that investigative phone call or other playful, serious, or adventurous first step. The first step is often the hardest, so make it teeny tiny if you need to. Even dipping in a toe will start a new flow. To prime the pump, you may want to brainstorm a whole page list of what would move your passion forward. Then pick one small, medium, or giant step that is ripe to take first. Just one.

  Sometimes to find your next step, you have to press the "master reset" button to not box yourself in by how you may have tried a similar move before. A new approach must surface, a fresh wave must rise up from the inside. Feel in, then decide what your next step might be.

  Let me make a feeling-based argument for staying in the moment, for taking action one step at a time. Planning too many steps ahead actually boxes you in. Can you feel that? Can you feel how your heart lifts as a plan begins to form, but drops when the planning gets too planned? Can you feel that by outlining every single aspect of how you're going to accomplish something (and closing to the possibility of any other way) that you actually don't have the internal room to invite a new (perhaps fresher, better, easier, or downright miraculous) way to appear? The more room you have inside, the bigger your possibilities outside.

Now, feel this, the movement of this exercise. We have a way-out-there or little tiny dream. We even have many, if not all, of the steps identified of how we're going to make it happen. But we loosen up our energetic grip on all but the next step that's in front of us in this very moment—both leaving room for new ideas to enter, and allowing us to use our full concentration of what's in front of us right now. We're efficient and creative. Organized and open. What a fresh and rewarding place to be: full steam ahead, while open to possibility!

- **ARE YOU REALLY, REALLY, REALLY INSPIRED TO DO THIS RIGHT NOW?** With inspiration, a delectable, infectious tension builds, giving you energy to take that next step, culminating in that letter going out, phone call being made, chapter being written, program firmed up, or audition scheduled—and nailed with a little punch-through. And even if you don't immediately get what you want, you can enjoy the warm stretch of your muscles and the tingling stimulation of your cells, and be completely, utterly, and undeniably satisfied that you went for it, that you passionately rode your soul's wave.

  Tell me, are you inspired to take that step you've identified—*today?*

7. movement is mandatory. Our energetic muscles are strong enough, and we have the basic dance moves (open, close, dive, fly, soar) down well enough to try a few combinations. Flexibility, agility, and fine-tuning are the goals of this game. Feel each of the following to the best of your ability.

- **CIRCULAR SOAR.** Pretend you are soaring high in the sky, gracefully circling over an open field below, supported by the warm wind of a gentle thermal. Look with an expanded perspective at that thing you identified that you really, really, really want and the next step you identified to take. How do they look from here? Then with three simple flaps, effortless on your part, start the very same circle again.

- **CIRCULAR MOTION.** As you are taking another loop around that same circle, you notice a second warm thermal breeze rise up, another of life's options presenting itself. It intrigues you, so you turn toward it, flap three times with a calm vigor, then relax your wings and join with its force, traveling new ground.

- **CAT AND MOUSE.** Imagine that you see something of interest in the field below—a new idea, perhaps, or a person you'd like to know. Engage those mighty wings, following your piqued interest, focus, and go for what you really, really, really want. Do it with a passion. Do it with your inner force.

- **DEFLATE, INFLATE.** Pretend you're a helium balloon floating outside, set free from the hand of a child. Imagine yourself also set free from your own thoughts and concerns. The sun is out and warms up your helium, expanding it to be greater than any doubts and fears. You happily soar—then burst with joy.

- **CATCHER'S STANCE.** Imagine you are a catcher, arms in and forward, hands forming a cup. At the same time, open your chest, relax your sternum, and put your energetic feelers out wide to find the perfect person, idea, or timing to complete your pass.

- **PLANT THE SEED.** You're busy on one project and have another in the wings. Imagine that instead of ignoring the second one until the first one's done, you formulate its question in your mind, not searching for the answer in that moment, just opening to let the answer come. Plant the seed so your mind works subconsciously on the solution.

- **DEADLINE RUSH.** You're focused, rushing toward a big deadline. As you are moving, keep a part of yourself open wide, calmly scanning for new possibilities or mid-course corrections that can take you even farther—faster.

- **QUICK SHIFT.** You're moving forward at a decent clip and keeping really, really, really open at the same time. BAM, a new idea enters. Following this new wind's flow, you instantly change direction and gear up for the next updraft. POW!

- **FOCUSED PLUNGE.** You've taken a clear, pure leap off a cliff's edge into the new, delighting in the wind's force filling your wings. Then slowly over time, you go back to your habit of flap, flap, flapping, getting lost in the details, and trying to control each aspect of the outcome. But this time you catch yourself, it feels as silly to you as it does to me typing this. You reopen in full flight, concentrating on just your one next step, with a clear long-term vision, and relax about the unknown details that lie in between. Breathe.

- **THE WITCH'S BREW.** Someone says to you the equivalent of, "Get out! And don't return until you've brought back the broomstick from the Wicked Witch of the West!" You feel hurt, dejected, rejected, and confused. Then after the door slams behind you and you dust off your clothes, you look up. Your vision opens, your heart stirs, and the help you need for the next part of the journey appears.

- **FEEDBACK.** Pretend you have to give some people feedback and are nervous about it. You begin to shrink, wondering how they'll react to what you're planning to say. Now press that "master reset" button, take a good breath, and approach them again—"expanded" this time. Can you feel that by you staying open, it's easier for them to be open, too?

- **MULTI-TASK.** Pretend you are doing three to five things at once: talking on the phone, pushing the trash can into position with your foot, writing something down, and listening for the doorbell, for example. Now, slow down the motion in your mind and concentrate on the subtle openings that occur as you shift from one task to another in your full-scale juggle.

- **WHAT A HEADACHE!** With an imaginary ache in your head, open your mind wide instead of resisting the pressure. Invite a gentle breeze in and feel the tension dissipate.

- **HANGING AROUND.** Pretend you don't know your role or how you fit in. Sit with uncertainty on the branch of a tree—not letting it drain the least bit of energy from you. Kick back. Relax. Enjoy the view just the same.

- **POWER-WAIT.** Put your awareness both in your innermost core and the outermost reaches of your galaxy at same time. Remain silent, open, graceful, expectant. No flapping or yakking allowed.

8. let's dance. Now that our energetic muscles are toned, let's try some of the specific steps that I used during the creation of this book.

- **LOSE THE BOREDOM.** Sometimes being bored is a sign that it's no longer good for you to continue doing something or it's not the right time to be doing it—or both. When I hit a writer's block, a red flag went up to my colleague. She suggested that I throw away any steps that felt the least bit old, dull, or done before. Can you get rid of any "steps" you have like this (boring habits, predictable reactions, worn-out activities, old vices, etc.)? Is it time?

- **STRETCH TO THE NEW.** *"Pretend your book is still being read one hundred years from now,"* my friend said. *"Think big, and bigger yet. Really, really, really stretch."* It's your turn now. Take the lid off your box. Heck, throw the walls away, too. Take that thing you say you want and pump it way, way up. Think big, bigger, and biggest yet. See what new energy this opens up.

- **PARTNER WITH THE ENERGY.** As I was writing the first manuscript drafts, I could tell you exactly which stories I'd used, which points I'd made, and practically which page they were on. But by the final draft, as the book took life, I could no longer plan what I was going to write, outline chapters in advance, or even remember which examples I'd put where. The book wrote itself alongside me.

  To partner with your passion, begin by making friends with it. Talk to it. Is it resting today or raring to go? Do you have a good feeling about where the two of you are headed—a confidence, a smile? Let your imagination tell you the answers.

9. we're constantly changing. Creation demands that change happen, which means we constantly have to "re-know" ourselves and each other.

- **UNKNOW YOURSELF.** To make space for the new, let's let go of old ideas we've had of ourselves. Take my book, for example, and its old 450-page-expose-every-detail-of-my-flight version. This new draft, two chapters of personal story plus eight steps, is both more respectful of me and more helpful to you. Cleaner, lighter, clearer . . . with even more power.

   Write a list of the things that have changed about you since you started reading this book—yes, belly-buttons and attitudes count. Then change *one thing* in your favorite room that better reflects the "you" that you are now, or open your mind to *one new way* that something you are planning will be accomplished. One small, medium, or big thing will do just fine.

- **LET THEM CHANGE.** In college, a friend once chastised me for locking one of our friends in a metaphoric box. "He's a different person than he was before, Sally. *Let him change!*" Before that moment, I hadn't appreciated the power that a small view on my part could have over someone else. Has this ever happened to you, from either angle? Overachievers, create a new bumper sticker or sign for the fridge: *"Let change happen."* Let change happen both to us, and to them.

- **LET THEM RECOGNIZE THEMSELVES THROUGH YOUR RECOGNITION OF THEM.** When you have a bigger view of people than they have of themselves, why not let them see what you see? Think of a person (or persons) who are beating themselves up right now. Now without saying a word out loud, hold them as "already fixed," bigger than that smashed-up state they are in. This is a little stronger than "holding out hope" and a little less than "holding onto an ideal." It's a recognition not just of their potential, but of the jewel inside of them that *already exists*. The next time you see them, you can communicate this to them with words if you'd like, or simply through your attitude. One warning here: any concrete change has to be their choice to make.

10. break-up or break-through? Pretend you feel a rush of constructively "destructive" passion brewing: an anger, outburst, or annoyance on the move. How can you tell if it's time to *break-up* or *break-through?* Whether it's aimed at the office, home, friendship, volunteer post, or a hobby, don't assume it's time for a break-up, for letting that person or activity go. Maybe the energy just wants to spur you to have a conversation or instigate a change. Two people willing to be both open and engaged in forward movement is what's required. Ready, willing, and able—all three. Do you have a "break-up" or "break-through" situation that you're facing now?

11. power-wait. Let's develop a new relationship with waiting, making it a force that works for us rather than something that just annoys us. Relax and open to the following:

- **DROP THE RUSH.** Go twenty-four hours without rushing for even one minute. I dare you.
- **CREATE SPACE.** Push out at least one deadline. Better yet, four.
- **GIVE THEM SPACE.** If you're working, living, or playing with other people, open your heart and mind that magical half degree to give them space to spread their wings and add their unique touch.

12. picture it happening. Get out those crayons and color the house that you see on the next page. If you notice, the walls don't quite touch the roof. Don't worry, the reason will soon become clear.

- **UNDER THE HOUSE,** write the people, stuff, and experiences that form your foundation—the five most important to you (usually friends, family, homes, hobbies, jobs, pets, etc.).

- **ABOVE THE ROOF,** write your long-term vision, that thing you identified that you really, really, really want, like "raising my kids well," "getting that promotion," or "being happy." If you don't have a specific goal, write the general area that you are passionate about, like "family" or "technology."

- **BY THE THREE-FOOT-TALL WALLS,** write the next step or two that you can take in that direction, circling the one that's the ripest for action. It's easy to get intimidated by a goal that seems far away. So we want to concentrate on the very next step that is in front of us right now. If you're raising a family, for example, are the kids newborns or adolescents? Is your next step to help them to sleep through the night or to help them go after their dreams? If it's to get them to sleep through the night, is your next step to feed them more at dinnertime, put relaxing lavender oil in their bathwater, or something else?

- **THEN IN THE OPEN SPACE WHERE THE WALLS AREN'T FORMED YET,** write those unknowns, those things you're not sure about—like how you are going to finance school, or find the right partner for whatever lifestyle you'd like to live or whatever business or hobby that you want to do.

- **NOW TAKE A BIG STEP BACK** and get comfortable with the whole picture. Using your breath, let any tension about the amount of work or number of unknowns fly by, and open to the possibility of ease.

- **OVERACHIEVERS,** add two or more stories to the house. Really, really, really stretch your dream. And like before, identify just the next few steps you need to take toward it, circling the first of those to take right away. Don't fret about any unknown particulars of how your dream will come true. Think really, really, really *big,* and if need be, start very, very, very *small*— one step at a time.

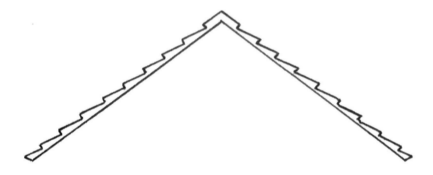

13. write to me. Or to anyone else you'd like. My only suggestion is that you do it three days in a row, and hold off mailing the letters until the week is through. Each letter should have three paragraphs, starting with:

- *My big, bigger, biggest, way-out-there dream is . . .*
- *The action step before me in this exact moment, right now, is . . .*
- *The detail that I've yet to figure out (and that I'm losing patience waiting for) is . . .*

Try it and see what happens. Chances are you'll figure out the answers for yourself. Don't be surprised if they come dancing right in! Still write to me, even if they do.

14. a final salutation. As my dear *Zio Giovannino,* the hub of our Sicilian family wheel, would say: *"Arrivederci,"* until we meet again! Then with his kind eyes shining, he would take your right hand in his, add his left to its other side to form a firm, pleasant hold, and look you gently in the eyes. For the kisses on each cheek, he would start with the right, then move to the left. His heartfelt gaze would then return, punctuated by a final squeeze of your hand. Try this yourself, twice in a row if you'd like. Feel the respect, celebration, and honor that passes from one person to the next. Help yourself to yourself . . . and each other. Today.

wrap-up

Life is a wonderful thing, even when it's not. I firmly believe that. Each of us has a purpose for being here, one or more effortless, natural gifts that sometimes drive us to do the hardest of work, and at other times steer us to hang out on the branch of a tree for a bit. A belief in ourselves and a relaxed open stance are two of the secrets to unleashing the passion for living that wants to pop out. And this passion, for me, is what life's all about.

I dream of a day when people will, in their own special way, feel *ready, willing, and able* to show their full selves to the world. And my next teeny tiny step toward that goal, you ask? To finish editing this chapter so I can publish my book. The unknown pieces? Whether adding my voice in print will serve the world somehow. And whether anyone other than my editor and my mom will get what I'm trying to say.

We've come a long way since the first pages of this book. We've put words to the seemingly random variety of feelings that the average human has inside, and (hopefully) formed at least one small piece of a quilt that we can call human consciousness. We've seen the way our feelings are doing the best they can to guide us, to serve as vocal chords of our soul, the world's soul, and the soul of what wants to be born in one of our tomorrows. We've experienced how we can access this inner wisdom to rise above the struggle and strife, and get real control over our days. We've felt a flexible, fluid control that's alive with movement, passion, and grace. And perhaps the most wonderful thing of all, with a little luck, we've felt the glimmer of peace that can fill us when the feeling nature of a genuinely imperfect human being is viewed as magical (and relevant) to modern day life.

I'm confident in humanity. That we'll know ourselves and harness our deepest passions to serve each other. That we'll join forces and unite. That we'll know when to reach in for answers and when to reach out. And that we'll laugh when we get it all wrong for a spell. I hope that by playing with the eight steps in this book, you are a little more confident, too, as well as more driven both to let your dreams out and to share them with the rest of us. We're waiting—*for you.*

invitation to play

A full wattage glow isn't just for closed-eye meditations, church services, or children anymore. It's available to all of us who want it . . . in our everyday lives. To people who are willing to say *"Hell, yes!"* to themselves, and move with what's right with the world.

Thank you for joining me in the experience of this book. If you want to keep up with the latest, connect with other like-souled people, or if you have something to say, come to the *www.comingtoyoursenses.com* Web site and connect. Overachievers, you'll find on-line support materials that you can use if you'd like to be a facilitator and experience soaring in groups. Express yourself. Fly. Be free.

cast of characters

best friend & devil's advocate	Jessica Stone Levy
right & left arms	Marla McDonald
	Jeanette Smith
directors of lighting	Soleira Green
	Helen Rockliff
sounding boards	Trudy Zachman
	Amy Caruso
sculptor	Georgia Roberts
surgeon	Caroline Pincus
illustrations & cover	David Bohn
	Diana Davis
layout	Alyson Alexander
soul face	Chiara Perni

about the author

Sally M. Veillette was trained as an electrical engineer, and received her Bachelor of Science degree from Brown University with the highest honors and awards granted. For the next fourteen years, she worked in marketing, advertising, and management in the high technology field, most recently serving as vice president and general manager of an electronics manufacturing company in Redmond, Washington.

Sally has spent her last ten years studying the human soul, ironically being forced into the exploration through an illness that had no medical cure. She has traveled the world, teaching and exploring the approaches that various cultures use to connect inward, and has seen the ways that this inner connection influences outward choices and self-expression—both with individuals and groups.

Her work has taken her to many interesting places—from the bottom of the Grand Canyon to the top of Mount Kilimanjaro, from the halls of Stanford University to the auditorium of the women's correctional facility in Gig Harbor, Washington. An outdoor enthusiast, Sally has hiked, skied, or climbed most of the mountains in the Northwest, and several others around the world. When she is not traveling, Sally and her family split their time between homes in Seattle, Washington, and Italy.